Course
Part A **3**

Contemporary Mathematics in Context

A Unified Approach

CORE-PLUS MATHEMATICS PROJECT

Course 3 Part A

Contemporary Mathematics in Context
A Unified Approach

Arthur F. Coxford
James T. Fey
Christian R. Hirsch
Harold L. Schoen
Gail Burrill
Eric W. Hart
Ann E. Watkins
with
Mary Jo Messenger
Beth Ritsema

EVERYDAY LEARNING®

Chicago, Illinois

Cover images: Images © 1998 PhotoDisc, Inc.

Everyday Learning Development Staff

Editorial: Anna Belluomini, Eric Karnowski, Steve Mico, Carol Zacny

Production/Design: Fran Brown, Annette Davis, Héctor Cuadra, Norma Underwood

Additional Credits: Maureen Laude

This project was supported, in part, by the National Science Foundation.
The opinions expressed are those of the authors and not necessarily those of the Foundation.

ISBN 1-57039-578-0 (Part A)

ISBN 1-57039-582-9 (Part B)

Any questions regarding this policy should be addressed to:

Everyday Learning Corporation
P.O. Box 812960
Chicago, IL 60681

1 2 3 4 5 6 7 8 9 BP 02 01 00 99 98

Preface

Assessing what students know and are able to do is an integral part of the *Contemporary Mathematics in Context* curriculum. Opportunities for assessment occur in each phase of the instructional model, from the lesson launch discussions and follow-up investigations to the "Checkpoint" and "On Your Own" tasks. The MORE (Modeling, Organizing, Reflecting, and Extending) activities following the investigations provide another means for evaluating the level of understanding of each individual student. Methods for conducting these curriculum-embedded assessments include fundamental classroom techniques of observing, listening, and questioning. As the students work through each lesson, the teacher will have ample opportunity to observe and assess how the students think about and apply mathematics.

More formal assessment can also be made, and it is to that end that the materials in this resource book were created. For each unit, there are several different types of assessment activities presented here:

- Quizzes (two forms for each lesson)
- In-class exams (two forms for each unit)
- Take-home exam items (three for each unit)
- Projects (two for each unit)

Sample solutions are provided for the quizzes and in-class exams, and the take-home assessments include helpful teacher notes.

You may also want to refer to the *Contemporary Mathematics in Context Teacher's Guide*, which includes a valuable discussion of assessment and student evaluation. Among the topics presented are scoring assessments and assigning grades; both are topics of concern to all educators, especially to those who are implementing innovative teaching methods and mathematical content not typically taught in their classrooms.

Lesson 1 Quiz

1. Many people in sales jobs are not paid a fixed salary. Rather, they earn a commission based on a percentage of their total sales. Suppose that an encyclopedia salesperson's commission is recorded weekly, but the salesperson is paid every two weeks. The commission c that the salesperson will be paid depends on her sales for the first week x, her sales for the second week y, and her rate of commission r. The basic relation between these variables is given by the formula $c = rx + ry$.

   a. How much commission will the salesperson earn on sales of $2,500 one week and $2,850 the next week at 8% rate of commission? Explain your response.

   b. If the weekly sales are the same as in Part a, what rate of commission is required for the salesperson to earn at least $1,000 in commission? Show your work.

   c. If the rate of commission is 10%, the basic relation is $c = 0.1x + 0.1y$. Write an equation showing the second week's sales y as a function of the commission c and the first week's sales x. Explain.

Lesson 1 Quiz

d. If the first week's sales are $2,500 and the second week's sales are $2,850, the basic relation is $c = 2,500r + 2,850r$. Write an equation showing the rate of commission r as a function of the commission c. Show your work.

2. The speed of a bicycle S in feet per second is related to the number of revolutions of the crank per minute R, the circumference of the wheel C, the number of teeth on the front sprocket F, and the number of teeth on the back sprocket B:

$$S = \frac{CRF}{B}$$

a. If C is increased and R, F, and B remain constant, what happens to S? Explain your reasoning.

b. Solve for R in terms of C, S, F, and B. Explain how you obtained your equation.

3. Solve $y = 3x + 8z$ for x in terms of y and z. Then solve for z in terms of y and x. Show your work.

$x =$ _____ $z =$ _____

Suggested Solutions

1. **a.** $c = 0.08(2{,}500) + 0.08(2{,}850) = \$428$

    b. $1{,}000 = r(2{,}500 + 2{,}850) = 5{,}350r$
    $r = \frac{1{,}000}{5{,}350} \approx 0.187 \approx 18.7\%$

    c. $c = 0.1x + 0.1y$

$c - 0.1x = 0.1y$	Subtract $0.1x$.
$0.1y = c - 0.1x$	Exchange sides.
$y = \frac{c - 0.1x}{0.1}$	Divide by 0.1.

    or $y = \frac{c}{0.1} - x$

    d. $c = 2{,}500r + 2{,}850r$

$c = 5{,}350r$	Distributive property.
$5{,}350r = c$	Exchange sides.
$5{,}350r \div 5{,}350 = c \div 5{,}350$	Divide by 5,350.
$r = \frac{c}{5{,}350}$	

2. **a.** S will increase. Increasing C will increase the value of the numerator in the fraction. If the denominator remains the same, this will make the value of the fraction greater.

    b. $R = \frac{SB}{CF}$ first multiply both sides by B, and then divide both sides by CF.

3. Adding $-8z$ to both sides gives $y - 8z = 3x$. Switching sides and dividing both sides by 3 gives $x = \frac{y - 8z}{3}$. To solve for z, add $-3x$ to both sides, giving $y - 3x = 8z$. Switching sides and dividing both sides by 8 gives $z = \frac{y - 3x}{8}$.

Unit 1

Lesson 1 Quiz

Form B

1. A local store plans to stock up on notebooks before the fall school rush. From past experience, the manager, Vanessa, estimates that she could sell 20 small blue notebooks. The larger burgundy notebooks always seem to sell out. Her costs are $1.00 for the small notebook and $1.50 for the large notebook.

   a. Write a rule that expresses Vanessa's total cost C as a function of the costs for the small and large notebooks, S and L.

   b. Assuming that Vanessa orders 20 small notebooks and that $100 has been set aside for the purchase of notebooks, how many large burgundy notebooks can Vanessa order?

   c. Write an equation that expresses the number of large notebooks L that can be purchased as a function of the cost C and the number of small notebooks S ordered.

Lesson 1 Quiz

2. A person's weight in space S can be found by the formula $S = \frac{rw}{d}$, where r is the radius of the Earth, w is the person's weight on Earth, and d is the person's distance from the center of the Earth.

    a. How will a person's weight in space S change as the person moves farther away from the Earth's surface?

    b. Ron and Carlos are both in the space shuttle orbiting Earth. If Ron weighs more than Carlos when they are on Earth, what can you say about their weights in space? How does the formula help you determine this?

    c. Solve for d in terms of S, r, and w. Explain how you obtained your equation.

3. Express the relation $5x + 6y = 30$ in an equivalent form where y is a function of x. Show your work.

Suggested Solutions

1. **a.** $C = 1.00S + 1.50L$

    b. 53 large notebooks can be purchased. (The manager will have $0.50 left over.)

    c. $L = \frac{C - 1.00S}{1.50}$

2. **a.** As a person moves farther away from the Earth, the person's weight in space decreases.

    b. Ron weighs more than Carlos does in space also. If r and d are the same but w increases, then S increases also.

    c. $d = \frac{rw}{S}$: first multiply both sides by d and then divide both sides by S.

3. Add $-5x$ to both sides, giving $6y = 30 - 5x$. Divide both sides by 6, giving $y = \frac{30 - 5x}{6}$ or $y = 5 - \frac{5}{6}x$.

Lesson 2 Quiz

1. Melissa and Rosa are golfing on a beautiful summer day. The ninth hole is 380 yards. Melissa hooked (hit to the left of the correct direction) her drive on hole #9, as sketched below.

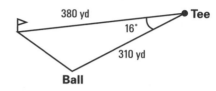

   How far is Melissa's ball from the hole? Explain or show your work.

2. A triangular region has sides measuring 25, 35, and 15 feet. Find the measure of the largest angle in the region.

3. Solve $\dfrac{a}{\sin A} = \dfrac{b}{\sin B}$ for a. Show your work.

Lesson 2 Quiz

4.   To know how much paint is needed for a barn, a farmer is estimating the total surface area of the barn. One part of the surface is triangular, as sketched below.

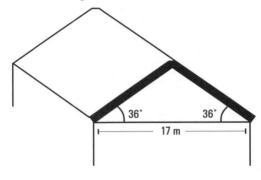

36°   36°
17 m

a.   The darkened sides in the figure are the edges of the roof. This trim will be painted white. Find the length of each of these two sides of the triangle. Explain or show your work.

b.   The triangular surface needs to be painted red. Find the area of the triangle. Explain or show your work.

   Use after page 45.

Suggested Solutions

1. $d^2 = 310^2 + 380^2 - 2(310)(380)\cos 16°$; $d \approx 118.4$ yards

2. $35^2 = 25^2 + 15^2 - 2(25)(15)\cos A$

   $\cos A = \frac{35^2 - 25^2 - 15^2}{-2(25)(15)}$

   $m\angle A = 120°$

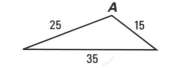

3. Multiply both sides by sin A, giving $a = \frac{b \sin A}{\sin B}$

4. **a.** The angle at the top is $180° - 2(36°)$ or $108°$. Using the Law of Sines, $\frac{d}{\sin 36°} = \frac{17}{\sin 108°}$; d ≈ 10.5 m.

   b. First, find the height of the triangle: $\sin 36° = \frac{h}{10.5}$, so $h = (\sin 36°)(10.5)$. Thus area $= 0.5(10.5)(\sin 36°)(17) \approx 52.5$ m^2.

Unit 1

Lesson 2 Quiz

Unit 1

1. Angie has 40 meters of fencing to use to create a safe play area for her baby brother.

   a. Angie wants to make the play area in the shape of a triangle, so she builds as shown below. Is it a right triangle? Show or explain your work.

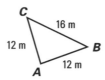

   b. Find the measure of angle *A*.

2. Solve $\dfrac{a}{\sin A} = \dfrac{b}{\sin B}$ for *b*. Show your work.

Lesson 2 Quiz

3. In parallelogram *ABCD*, *BD* = 12 m, m∠*A* = 75°, and m∠*BDA* = 45°.

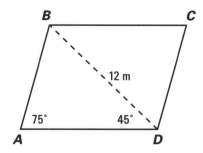

a. Find the length of side *AB*.

b. Find the area of the parallelogram.

Unit 1

Suggested Solutions

1. **a.** No. If this were a right triangle, then by the Pythagorean Theorem $12^2 + 12^2$ would equal 16^2. But $12^2 + 12^2 = 288$, and $16^2 = 256$.

    b. Use the Law of Cosines to find $m\angle A$.
    $\cos A = \frac{12^2 + 12^2 - 16^2}{2(12)(12)} \approx 0.111$. Therefore, $m\angle A \approx 83.6°$.

2. Multiply both sides by $\sin B$ giving $(\sin B)\left(\frac{a}{\sin A}\right) = b$, or $b = \frac{a \sin B}{\sin A}$.

3. **a.** $\frac{AB}{\sin 45°} = \frac{12}{\sin 75°}$

    $AB \approx 8.8$ m

    b. $\sin 60° = \frac{h}{8.8}$

    $h = 8.8\sin 60° \approx 7.6$

    area $ABCD = 2(\text{area } \triangle ABD)$

    $\approx 2\left(\frac{1}{2}\right)(12)(7.6)$

    ≈ 91.2 m^2

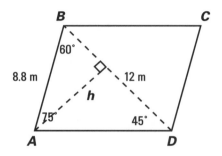

© 1999 Everyday Learning Corporation

Lesson 3 Quiz

Form A

1. The junior class of a small high school was planning a class party after the prom that would include a breakfast. The students got three bids from local restaurants.

   ■ Yolanda's Restaurant bid a flat rate of $15 per person.

   ■ The Fireside Inn bid a rental fee of $200, plus $5 per person for food and service.

   ■ Suttmiller's Restaurant bid a rental fee of $120, plus $10 per person for food and service.

   a. Write an equation showing how the total cost *c* of the class party at each restaurant would depend on the number of people *p* who attend.

   Yolanda's Restaurant: _____

   Fireside Inn: _____

   Suttmiller's Restaurant: _____

   b. Display graphs to illustrate the situation for the three restaurants. Label each axis with units, and explain what each variable and each axis represents.

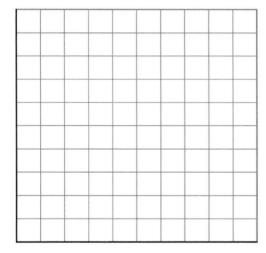

   c. Explain which restaurant you would choose under these conditions and why.

Lesson 3 Quiz

Unit 1

2. Each year, the Metropolis Supers professional softball team hosts a game in which all-stars from area high schools play the Supers. Based on data from previous years, the general manager decided that the income and operating costs can be represented as functions of ticket price according to the following equations and graph:

Income from ticket sales I is related to ticket price P by the equation $I = 500P - 50P^2$. Cost C of operating the game is related to ticket price P by the equation $C = 900 - 70P$.

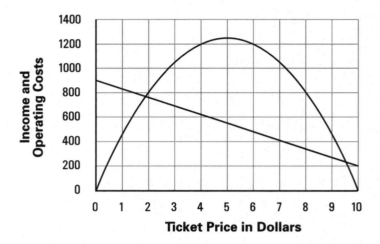

a. What ticket price(s) would generate the greatest income? What is the greatest income? Explain how you obtained your answers.

Ticket price(s):_____ Greatest income: _____

b. For what ticket price(s) would the operating costs be equal to the income from ticket sales? Explain how you obtained your answer.

3. Solve $14 + 5x > 6 + 3.5x$. Explain your method.

Use after page 62.

Suggested Solutions

1. **a.** Yolanda's Restaurant: $c = 15p$

    Fireside Inn: $c = 200 + 5p$

    Suttmiller's Restaurant: $c = 120 + 10p$

    b. The x-axis represents the number of people and the y-axis represents the cost in dollars.

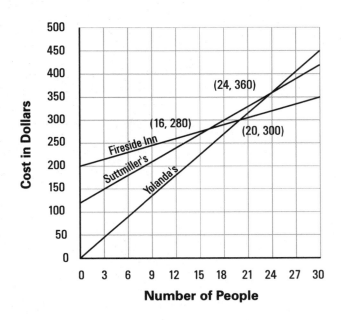

    c. The least expensive bid is Yolanda's, if there are fewer than 20 people attending. If there are more than 20, the Fireside Inn is least expensive. Suttmiller's is between these two, except when 16 to 24 people attend. Then it is the most expensive. At the point of intersection (20, 300), either Yolanda's or the Fireside Inn could be used.

2. **a.** The highest point of the parabola is the desired solution. The ticket price is $5 and the maximum income is $500(5) - 50(5^2)$, or $1,250.

    b. The points of intersection of the line (operating expenses) and parabola (income) are the solutions. Either the graph or table on a calculator or computer software gives ticket prices of about $1.89 and $9.51.

3. $x > -5.33$ or $x > -\frac{16}{3}$

    Students might find this solution using graphs, tables of values, or symbolic reasoning.

Name _____ Date _____

Unit 1

1. Curtis's parents decided to throw a graduation party for him and a few of his friends. They inquired at some restaurants, and they were given the following costs for separate "event rooms."

   The first would charge $400 for the evening.

   The second would charge $250, plus $5 for each person in attendance.

   The third would charge $200, plus $10 for each person in attendance.

   a. Write an equation showing how the cost c of reserving the event room would depend on the number of people p who attend.

   Restaurant #1: _____

   Restaurant #2: _____

   Restaurant #3: _____

   b. Display graphs to illustrate the situation for the three restaurants. Label each axis with units and explain what each variable and each axis represents.

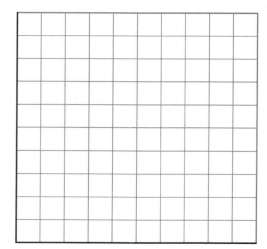

   c. Explain which restaurant you would choose under different conditions and why.

Lesson 3 Quiz

2. Each year, the combined high school orchestras in Muse City stage a public concert. Based on data from previous years, the organizers decided that the income and operating costs can be represented as functions of ticket price according to the following equations and graph: Income from ticket sales I is related to ticket price P by the equation $I = 500P - 50P^2$. Cost C of operating the concert is related to ticket price P by the equation $C = 600 - 50P$.

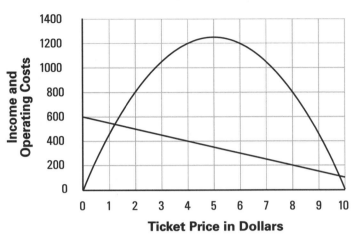

a. What ticket price(s) would generate the greatest income? What is the greatest income? Explain how you obtained your answer.

   Ticket price(s): _____   *Greatest income:* _____

b. For what ticket price(s) would the operating costs be equal to the income from ticket sales? Explain how you obtained your answer.

3. Solve $12 + 6x < 8 + 1.5x$. Explain your method.

Suggested Solutions

1. **a.** Restaurant #1: $c = 400$

    Restaurant #2: $c = 250 + 5p$

    Restaurant #3: $c = 200 + 10p$

    b. The x-axis represents the number of people and the y-axis represents the cost in dollars.

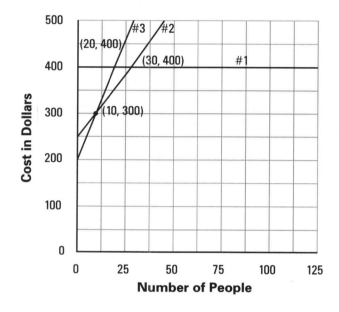

    c. It is clear from the graph that restaurant #1 is least expensive if more than 30 people attend, restaurant #2 is least expensive if between 10 and 30 people attend, and restaurant #3 is least expensive if fewer than 10 people attend. At the intersection points, either of the two restaurants whose prices intersect could be used. Of course, factors other than cost may be important, but we have no information on that.

2. **a.** The highest point of the parabola is the desired solution. The ticket price is $5, and the maximum income is $500(5) - 50(5^2)$, or $1,250.

    b. The points of intersection of the line (operating expenses) and parabola (income) are the solutions. Either the graph or table on a calculator or computer software gives ticket prices of about $1.23 and $9.77.

3. $x < -0.89$ or $x < -\frac{8}{9}$
    Students might find this solution using graphs, tables of values, or symbolic reasoning.

Lesson 4 Quiz

1. The Fun & Games Company produces two kinds of water pistols, regular and long distance. The company can make at most 600 regular and 400 long-distance water pistols per week.

   a. Write and graph inequalities expressing the given constraints on water pistol manufacturing.

      Inequalities: _____

      _____

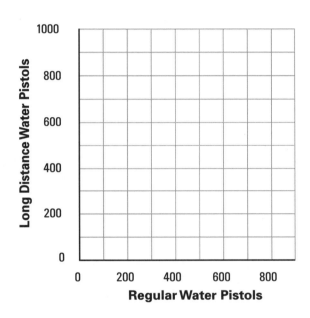

   b. Suppose the total number of water pistols manufactured in a week cannot exceed 900. What inequality would express this constraint? Graph this new constraint on the coordinate axis above.

      Inequality: _____

Unit 1

c. Suppose the company will realize a profit of $1 on each regular water pistol and $1.20 on each long-distance water pistol. Write the profit function.

d. How many of each product should the company make to get maximum profit? Show your work.

2. Consider the linear equation $3x + 2y = 6$.

a. Describe two methods for graphing this equation. Sketch the graph. Be sure to designate the scale on your axes.

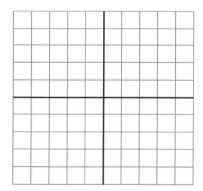

b. On the graph in Part a, show the region where points have coordinates satisfying the inequality $3x + 2y \geq 6$.

Suggested Solutions

1. **a.** $x \le 600$ and $y \le 400$ where x is the number of regular water pistols and y is the number of long-distance water pistols. The third constraint graphed below is given in Part b.

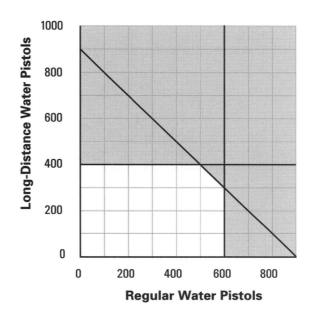

b. $x + y \le 900$

See graph above.

c. $P = x + 1.2y$

d. 500 regular water pistols and 400 long-distance water pistols. The vertices of the feasible region are (0, 0), (600, 0), (0, 400), (500, 400) and (600, 300). The vertex (500, 400) yields a higher profit.

Suggested Solutions *(continued)*

2. **a.** One method is to plot two or three ordered pairs that satisfy the given equation, say (0, 3), (2, 0), and (4, −3). Then draw the line that contains these points. A second method is to rewrite the given equation using an equivalent form in which y is a function of x; that is, $y = -1.5x + 3$. Then graph this function with a calculator or by using the slope-intercept approach.

The region marked below is the solution to Part b.

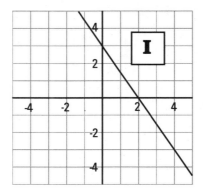

    b. Ordered pairs of points on the line and in Region I satisfy $3x + 2y \geq 6$.

Lesson 4 Quiz

Form B

1. The Fine Threads Company produces regular and v-neck T-shirts. The company can make at most 500 regular and 400 v-neck T-shirts per week.

   a. Write and graph inequalities expressing the given constraints on T-shirt manufacturing.

   Inequalities: _____

   _____

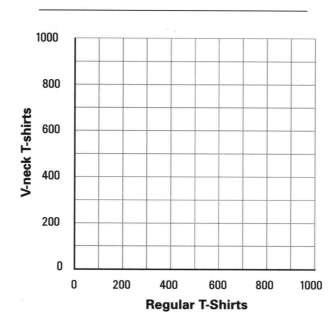

   b. Suppose the total number of T-shirts manufactured in a week cannot exceed 800. What inequality would express this constraint? Graph this new constraint on the coordinate axis above.

   Inequality: _____

Unit 1

c. Suppose the company will realize a profit of 30 cents on each regular T-shirt and 50 cents on each v-neck T-shirt. Write the profit function.

d. How many of each product should the company make to get maximum profit? Explain.

2. Consider the linear equation $2x + 3y = 6$.

a. Describe two methods for graphing this equation. Sketch the graph. Be sure to designate the scale on your axes.

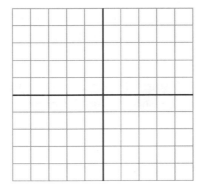

b. On the graph in Part a, show the region where points have coordinates satisfying the inequality $2x + 3y \leq 6$.

Suggested Solutions

1. **a.** $x \leq 500$ and $y \leq 400$ where x is the number of regular T-shirts and y is the number of v-neck T-shirts. The third constraint graphed below is given in Part b.

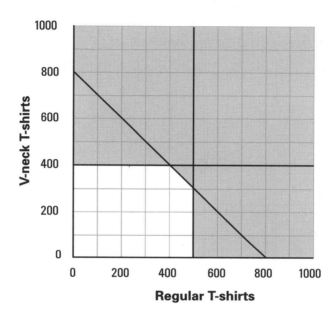

    b. $x + y \leq 800$

    See graph above.

    c. $P = 30x + 50y$ It should be noted that this is the profit in cents. Students may set up the equation $P = 0.30x + 0.50y$ in which the profit would be in dollars.

    d. 400 regular and 400 v-neck T-shirts. The vertices of the feasible region are (0, 0), (0, 400), (500, 0), (400, 400), and (500, 300). The vertex (400, 400) yields a higher profit.

Unit 1

Suggested Solutions *(continued)*

2. **a.** One method is to plot two or three ordered pairs that satisfy the given equation, say (0, 2), (3, 0), and (–3, 4). Then draw the line that contains these points. A second method is to rewrite the given equation using an equivalent form in which y is a function of x, that is, $y = -\frac{2}{3}x + 2$. Then graph this function with a calculator or by using the slope-intercept approach.

The region marked below is the solution to Part b.

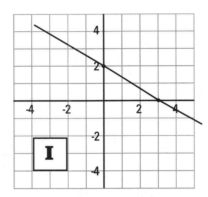

b. Ordered pairs of points on the line and in Region I satisfy $2x + 3y \le 6$.

In-Class Exam

1. The loudness L of the sound of a stereo speaker at a concert varies inversely as the square of the listener's distance d from the speaker.

    a. Which of these equations might represent the relationship between L and d, where k is a constant depending on the units of L and d? Explain.

    $$L = kd^2 \qquad L = \frac{k}{d^2} \qquad L = \frac{k}{d}$$

    b. As you move farther away from the speaker, the loudness decreases. How is this reflected in the equation you chose in Part a?

    c. The relationship between L and d for a speaker at a concert in Ravenna Park is given by $Ld^2 = 1{,}273$. Write an equivalent equation that gives L as a function of d. Explain how you used the properties of equality.

In-Class Exam

Unit 1

2. The Back-to-the-Basics Ice Cream Company makes two flavors, vanilla and chocolate. Each day, the company can make up to 1,000 quarts of ice cream, and the sales department can sell up to 800 quarts of vanilla and up to 600 quarts of chocolate.

   a. Write a system of inequalities representing these constraints on the number of quarts of vanilla v and chocolate c that the company can manufacture and sell.

   b. Use the grid below to find the feasible region for the system of inequalities in Part a. Clearly label the axes.

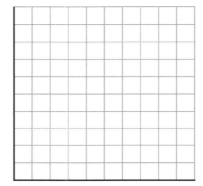

   c. Past sales data suggest that in the first quarter of the year, the Back-to-the-Basics profit is 10 cents per quart for vanilla and 13 cents per quart for chocolate. Find the number of quarts of each kind of ice cream to produce in the first quarter for the maximum daily profit. Explain or show your work.

In-Class Exam

3. Jenna needs to have some electrical outlets installed in her house. She contacts two different companies and obtains the following information:

Brown Electric charges $80 for the trip and $40 for installing each electrical outlet. Zap Electric charges $20 for the trip and $50 for installing each electrical outlet.

a. Write equations that will give the total charge for each company as a function of the number of outlets installed.

b. Under what conditions should Jenna choose Zap Electric to do the work? Explain how you found your answer.

c. Using a method of your choice, solve the following inequality and explain what question in the given situation could be answered by the solution.

$$80 + 40x \leq 1,000$$

4. The Law of Cosines and the Law of Sines can be used to find missing parts of triangles, when at least three parts are given. If the measures of two angles and the length of the included side are known, explain how to find the other side lengths and angle measure. Be sure to indicate when and how the Law of Cosines or Law of Sines is used.

5. The sides of a triangular lot in a subdivision have measures of 50 meters, 40 meters, and 35 meters.

   a. Find the degree measure of the smallest angle. Show or explain your work.

   b. Find the area of the lot to the nearest square meter. Show or explain your work.

Use after page 90.

© 1999 Everyday Learning Corporation

Unit 1

Suggested Solutions

1. **a.** $L = \frac{k}{d^2}$; this is the only one of the given equations that represents L varying inversely as the square of d.

   b. In the equation, increasing d increases the denominator of the fraction, and so the overall value of L is decreased.

   c. To write L as a function of d, divide both sides by $d^2 \cdot L = \frac{1,273}{d^2}$

2. **a.** Manufacturing: $v + c \leq 1,000$
      Sales: $v \leq 800$ and $c \leq 600$

   b.

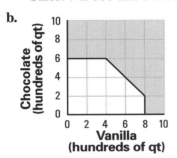

   c. The profit function is $P = 10v + 13c$, where P is in cents. The corners of the feasible region are the points to check, but only (400, 600) or (800, 200) make sense, since these points clearly will yield greater profit than (0, 600) and (800, 0), respectively. Testing them, $P = 10(400) + 13(600) = 11,800$ at (400, 600) and $P = 10(800) + 13(200) = 10,600$ at (800, 200). Thus, the best choice is 400 quarts of vanilla and 600 quarts of chocolate.

3. **a.** Let C represent the total cost and x represent the number of outlets installed.

   Brown Electric: $C = 80 + 40x$
   Zap Electric: $C = 20 + 50x$

   b. Students may use tables, graphs, or symbolic reasoning to get the solution to the inequality $20 + 50x < 80 + 40x$. The two lines intersect at (6, 320). So Zap Electric is cheaper if Jenna needs to have fewer than 6 outlets installed. Both companies charge the same price for installing 6 outlets.

   c. The solution to the inequality is $x \leq 23$. The question that could be answered by this inequality is, how many outlets can be installed by Brown Electric without the cost exceeding $1,000?

Unit 1

Suggested Solutions *(continued)*

4. The measure of the third angle is 180° minus the sum of the two given angles. Use the Law of Sines to find the length of a second side and either Law to find the length of the third side.

5. **a.** $\cos^{-1} \left(\frac{50^2 + 40^2 - 35^2}{2 \cdot 50 \cdot 40} \right) \approx 44°$

   b. $height \approx 40 \cdot \sin 44°$
   $Area \approx 0.5 \cdot 50 \cdot 40 \cdot \sin 44°$
   ≈ 695 square meters

In-Class Exam

1. The resistance R of an electrical wire is related to the specific resistance K of the wire material, the length L of the wire, and the cross-sectional area A of the wire. The formula is $R = \frac{KL}{A}$.

   a. How is the resistance R affected for the following changes in the other variables? Explain.

   Increase of the specific resistance of wire material K:

   Decrease in the length L:

   Decrease in the cross-sectional area A:

   b. Write an equation that gives L as a function of A, K, and R and is equivalent to the given equation. Explain your procedure.

2. The Colonel Mills Cereal Company has on hand 800 pounds of oats and 40 pounds of sugar. They can make a box of Healthios from 0.5 pound of oats and no sugar. They can make a box of Tastios from 0.4 pound of oats and 0.1 pound of sugar.

   a. Write a system of inequalities representing these constraints on the number of boxes of Healthios H and Tastios T that the company can make.

Unit 1

In-Class Exam

b. Use the grid below to find the feasible region for the system of inequalities in Part a. Clearly label the axes.

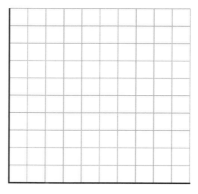

c. Past summer-sales data suggest that the company's profit per box is 10 cents for Healthios and 13 cents for Tastios. Find the number of boxes of each kind of cereal to produce for the maximum daily profit this summer, if the sales pattern remains the same as in past summers. Explain or show your work.

3. a. Solve $20x + 15 \leq 10x + 85$.

Show or explain how you obtained your solution.

b. Explain how to solve the same inequality using a different method than you used in Part a.

In-Class Exam

4. The Law of Cosines and the Law of Sines can be used to find missing parts of triangles when at least three parts are given. If the lengths of all three sides are known, explain how to find the measures of all three angles. Be sure to indicate when and how the Law of Cosines or Law of Sines is used.

5. Folleta wanted to hike from point *P* to point *R*, but because of impassable marshland, she hiked from *P* to *T* and then to *R*.

   a. The length of *PT* is 1.1 km. Find *TR*. Explain or show your work.

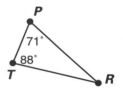

   b. Find how far off course Folleta hiked; that is, find the perpendicular distance from *T* to line *PR*. Show your work.

Unit 1

Suggested Solutions

1. **a.** *R* increases in the first and third cases and decreases in the second case.

    b. To write *L* as a function of *A*, *K*, and *R*, multiply both sides by *A*, and then divide both sides by *K*. $L = \frac{RA}{K}$

2. **a.** Oats: $0.5H + 0.4T \le 800$

    Sugar: $0.1T \le 40$

    b.

    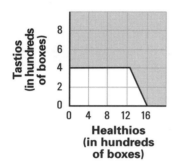

    c. The profit function is $P = 10H + 13T$, where *P* is in cents. The corners of the feasible region are the points to check, but only (1280, 400) or (1600, 0) make sense, since (1280, 400) will clearly yield greater profit than (0, 400). Testing them, $P = 10(1,280) + 13(400) = 18,000$ at (1280, 400), and $P = 10(1,600) + 13(0) = 16,000$ at (1600, 0). Thus, the best choice is 1,280 boxes of Healthios and 400 boxes of Tastios.

3. **a–b.** $x \le 7$

    Students could solve this algebraically, graphically, or using tables of values.

4. Use the Law of Cosines to find one angle, then either Law to find a second one. The third angle is 180° minus the sum of the first two.

5. **a.** Use the Law of Sines. $\frac{1.1}{\sin 21°} = \frac{TR}{\sin 71°}$; $TR \approx 2.9$ km

    b. Let *d* be the perpendicular distance from *T* to line *PR*. Then $\sin 71° = \frac{d}{1.1}$ or $d = 1.1 \sin 71° \approx 1.04$ km.

Take-Home Assessment

1. In this unit, variables were related in many ways. Recall how you used the terms *direct variation* and *indirect variation* in the Course 2 unit, "Power Models." You explored direct variation, inverse variation, and combined variation, where the combined variation could involve both direct and inverse variation. Look through this unit. Make a list that includes an example of each of the above kinds of variation, including as many different kinds of combined variation as you can. Describe at least two real-life situations that are not included in this unit, and illustrate one or more of these kinds of variation among variables.

2. Different types of relationships between variables that are in this unit are (a) several variables related by a single equation, (b) several equations with the same input variable, and (c) analysis by linear programming. Review problem situations from the unit that are examples of each of these types of relationships. Write a one- or two-page description of the characteristics of problems that fit into each of these categories.

3. Write a test that you think would adequately cover all of the important ideas in this unit. The test should be written at a level of difficulty that is appropriate for your classmates. Use the "Checkpoint" and "On Your Own" features as a guide. Your test should reflect the expectations for student learning in this unit. Provide an answer key and a guide for scoring your test.

Unit 1

1. This project could be done by one student working alone or by a pair of students. The purpose is to reinforce the meanings of different kinds of variation and to help students recognize instances of such variation in real-world situations. Real-world examples of such variation are numerous as the review of this unit should show.

2. Like the previous problem, this problem could be done by one student working alone or by a pair of students. It, too, could serve as a review for an in-class exam as well as an assessment itself. The purpose is to help students better see the types of relationships that may exist between multiple variables and to recognize various real-world situations as instances of some of these types of relationships.

3. This project also can be done by a student working alone or by pairs of students. The students' choice of test items will be a good indication of what they think is important and of their impression of what you think is important. Be flexible in your grading of this project. Base the grades on the consistency of what the students choose to do, the accuracy of solutions, and the completeness of coverage of the test. If time permits, it may be interesting to have other students complete a test constructed by classmates, followed by a class discussion of the test.

Project

More on Linear Programming

Purpose

Business and industry frequently use linear programming. For this reason, most advanced high school or beginning college textbooks on Business Mathematics or Finite Mathematics contain a chapter or two on linear programming. In this project, you will explore the treatment of the topic in some of these books and compare it to what is done in this unit.

Directions

1. Find two textbooks that have chapters on linear programming. Your teacher may be able to provide you with some sources, or use your school or community library. Business Mathematics or Finite Mathematics textbooks at the advanced high school or beginning college levels will be the best sources.

2. Skim the first few introductory sections on linear programming in these books. In particular, look for the way constraints, feasible sets, objective functions, and the solution methods are presented.

3. Compare the approach to each of these topics with Lesson 4 of this unit.

4. Write a report comparing how the two sources and Lesson 4 treat each of the topics: constraints, feasible sets, objective functions, and the solution methods. Begin your report with a short introduction in which you explain the goals of your project and how the report is organized. Write a few paragraphs for each topic that include problems or examples from your sources to illustrate the differences or similarities of approaches among the two sources and Lesson 4. End your report with a brief summary of the differences and similarities that you found in the three approaches that you compared. Include a discussion of what you learned about linear programming from this project.

Unit 1

More on Linear Programming

This project can best be done by pairs or small groups of students, as the group interaction should increase learning. It should provide students the opportunity to gain a deeper appreciation of linear programming, especially in business settings. Another goal is to give students experience finding and reading mathematical resources beyond their textbooks.

Suggested Timeline

Give a deadline for finding sources. This may not be easy, depending on what you have on hand or what is in your local or school library. If there is a college or community college nearby, students should be able to find appropriate sources in that library. Give two writing deadlines, one for submitting a rough draft of the report, to which you provide feedback and return to the students for rewriting, and a second deadline for submitting the report in its final form. Students should have from several days to a week to submit the first draft and at least a week more for the final report. In between, you might allow some class time for students to ask questions and to work on the reports.

Report Format

1. Introduction of the scope and purpose of the project including citation of the sources

2. Comparison of two sources and this unit relative to each linear programming topic

3. Examples or problems illustrating the differences and similarities

4. Summary of main differences and similarities and what new was learned

Suggested Evaluation Criteria

Inform the students of your criteria at the time that you make the assignment.

1.	Format of report follows directions	10%
2.	Clarity of introduction	10%
3.	Description of similarities and differences	30%
4.	Quality of examples	30%
5.	Clarity and accuracy of summary	20%

Project

Systems and Matrices: A Review

Purpose

Matrices, which you learned about in the Course 2 unit "Matrix Models," are a flexible mathematical tool, which can be used in a wide variety of settings. Lesson 3 of that unit was entitled "Matrices and Systems of Linear Equations." In this project, you will review how matrices are used in solving systems of equations, and compare that to what you have done in "Multiple-Variable Models."

Directions

1. Review the ways you have learned to solve systems of linear equations using matrices.

2. After reviewing this material, complete Investigation 3 of Lesson 4 in this unit, making use of matrix methods to solve the systems of equations whenever you can. Record your work to be included in a written report.

3. Choose any two of the five Modeling problems at the end of "Matrix Models," Lesson 3. Each gives a problem context that can be analyzed or solved with a system of linear equations. Rather than use matrix methods, as the problems ask, try to solve the problems using the methods in "Multiple-Variable Models." Again, neatly record your work.

4. Write a report that begins with a short introduction, in which you explain the goals of your project and how the report is organized. Next, include your work from Parts 2 and 3 above. End your report with a brief summary of the differences, similarities, strengths, and weaknesses that you found in the various approaches to solving systems of linear equations.

Unit 1

Systems and Matrices: A Review

Pairs or small groups of students should work together on this project. The review of matrices is an important goal, but perhaps more important is the broader goal of seeing the connectedness of mathematical ideas and methods. Solutions of the problems that are required in the project may not always be straightforward, since the problems were written with specific solution methods in mind. Emphasize to students that they should try to learn from the difficulties they encounter and from trying to understand why one problem poses a difficulty when one method is applied but is easy when another is applied. Note that Course 2, Part A textbooks must be made available to students for this project.

Suggested Timeline

Give students a few days to review the Matrix Models lesson. When they have completed the review, take some time to answer questions that may have arisen. To the extent that time permits, try to help them as they work on the investigations and problems as well. Give two writing deadlines, one for submitting a rough draft of the report to which you provide feedback and return to the students for rewriting, and a second deadline for submitting the report in its final form. Students should have from several days to a week to submit the first draft and at least a week for the final report. In between, you might allow some class time for students to ask questions and work on their reports.

Report Format

1. Introduction that states the goal and methods of the project

2. Record of the work on Investigation 3 of Lesson 4, using matrix methods

3. Solutions of the two problems from the "Matrix Models" lesson

4. Summary of differences, similarities, and relative strengths of different approaches

Suggested Evaluation Criteria

Inform the students of your criteria at the time you make the assignment.

1. Format of report follows directions   10%

2. Clarity and completeness of goals and methods description   10%

3. Quality of work on Investigation 3 of Lesson 4   25%

4. Quality of work on problems from the "Matrix Models" lesson   35%

5. Clarity and accuracy of summary comments   20%

Unit 1

Lesson 1 Quiz

1. A school club is planning to sell one kind of candy to raise funds. The members of the club narrowed the choices to candy bars, taffy, and jaw breakers. They then voted for their first, second, and third preferences. The outcome of the voting is given below.

Fund-Raiser Preference Table

	Rankings			
Candy Bars	1	2	3	1
Taffy	2	1	2	3
Jaw Breakers	3	3	1	2
Number of Voters	10	31	45	30

a. Using the plurality method, which type of candy, if any, is the winner? Explain.

b. Using the runoff method, which type of candy, if any, is the winner? Explain.

c. Using the pairwise-comparison method, which type of candy, if any, is the winner?

d. Using the points-for-preferences method, which type of candy, if any, is the winner?

e. Which type of candy should the club choose to sell to best reflect this vote? Explain your choice.

f. There can be different winners using different voting methods. Is there one particular method that always gives the fairest result?

Use after page 114.

Unit 2

Lesson 1 Quiz

Suggested Solutions

1. **a.** Using the plurality method, the winner is the candidate with the most first-preference votes. In this case, jaw breakers win with 45 first-preference votes.

    b. The runoff is between jaw breakers with 45 first preferences and candy bars with 40. Since candy bars are preferred over jaw breakers by 71 voters but jaw breakers are preferred by only 45 voters, candy bars are the runoff winner.

    c. Taffy is preferred to candy bars (76 to 40). Jaw breakers are preferred to taffy (75 to 41). Candy bars are preferred to jaw breakers (71 to 45). Therefore, there is no pairwise-comparison winner.

    d. Assigning 3 points for first preference, 2 for second, and 1 for third gives the following results:

    Candy bars: $10(3) + 31(2) + 45(1) + 30(3) = 227$

    Taffy: $10(2) + 31(3) + 45(2) + 30(1) = 233$

    Jaw breakers: $10(1) + 31(1) + 45(3) + 30(2) = 236$

    Jaw breakers, with the highest count, are the points-for-preference winner.

    e. Answers may vary, but probably the easiest choice to argue is jaw breakers, since it is both the plurality and the points-for-preferences winner. Furthermore, even though no method is perfect in situations in which there are more than two candidates (according to Arrow's Theorem), most experts recommend points-for-preferences or pairwise comparison. Since jaw breakers are the points-for-preferences winner and there is no pairwise-comparison winner, this is another argument supporting jaw breakers as the winner. Candy bars, on the other hand, beat jaw breakers in a runoff, so candy bars would be a plausible choice as well. Students should be given credit for this argument supporting candy bars. There does not seem to be a good argument for choosing taffy.

    f. No, not according to Arrow's formulation of fairness. Based on Arrow's definition of a fair voting method, Arrow's Theorem states that there is no voting method that will always yield a fair result when there are more than two candidates.

Unit 2

Lesson 1 Quiz

1. Charter High School just opened this year. Its first class voted for the school's mascot. The members of the class narrowed the choices to Rams, Tigers, and Eagles. They then voted for their first, second, and third preferences. The outcome of the voting is given below.

Mascot Preference Table

	Rankings			
Rams	2	1	2	3
Tigers	1	2	3	1
Eagles	3	3	1	2
Number of Voters	20	62	90	60

a. Using the plurality method, which mascot, if any, is the winner? Explain.

b. Using the runoff method, which mascot, if any, is the winner? Explain.

Unit 2

Lesson 1 Quiz

c. Using the pairwise-compairson method, which mascot, if any, is the winner? Explain.

d. Using the points-for-preferences method, which mascot, if any, is the winner? Explain.

e. Which mascot should the school choose to best reflect this vote? Exaplin your choice.

f. There can be different winners using different voting methods. Is there one particular method that always gives the fairest result?

© 1999 Everyday Learning Corporation

Lesson 1 Quiz

Suggested Solutions

1. **a.** Using the plurality method, the winner is the mascot with the most first-place votes. In this case, Eagles wins with 90 first-place votes.

    b. The runoff is between Eagles with 90 first preferences and Tigers with 80. Since Tigers is preferred over Eagles by 142 voters but Eagles is preferred by only 90 voters, Tigers is the runoff winner.

    c. Rams is preferred to Tigers (152 to 80). Tigers is preferred to Eagles (142 to 90). Eagles is preferred to Rams (150 to 82). Therefore, there is no pairwise-comparison winner.

    d. Assigning 3 points for first preference, 2 for second, and 1 for third gives the following results:

    Rams: $20(2) + 62(3) + 90(2) + 60(1) = 466$

    Tigers: $20(3) + 62(2) + 90(1) + 60(3) = 454$

    Eagles: $20(1) + 62(1) + 90(3) + 60(2) = 472$

    Eagles, with the highest count, is the points-for-preferences winner.

    e. Answers may vary, but probably the easiest choice to argue is Eagles, since it is both the plurality and the points-for-preferences winner. Furthermore, even though no method is perfect in situations in which there are more than two candidates (according to Arrow's Theorem), most experts recommend points-for-preferences or pairwise comparison. Since Eagles is the points-for-preferences winner and there is no pairwise-comparison winner, this is another argument supporting Eagles as the winner. Tigers, on the other hand, beats Eagles in a runoff, so Tigers would be a plausible choice as well. Students should be given credit for this argument supporting Tigers. There does not seem to be a good argument for choosing Rams.

    f. No, not according to Arrow's formulation of fairness. Based on Arrow's definition of a fair voting method, Arrow's Theorem states that there is no voting method that will always yield a fair result when there are more than two candidates.

Use after page 114.

Unit 2

Lesson 2 Quiz

1. For an assignment in social studies class, Panthong and Rylan used a survey to determine how much homework students in their school do. They selected a sample of 100 students to survey by choosing every fifth student leaving the building right after school. On their survey they asked, "How much homework do you usually do per day?"

   a. What is the population under investigation in this survey?

   b. Will Panthong and Rylan's procedure for selecting a sample produce a simple random sample?

   c. How could they conduct a census on this question?

   d. Do you think their survey design is biased? Explain your thinking.

   e. Suggest a better procedure.

Lesson 2 Quiz

Suggested Solutions

1. **a.** The population consists of all students in Panthong and Rylan's school.

    b. No, this is not a simple random sample, because not every group of 100 students has an equal chance of being selected. For example, if two students always leave the building together, at most one of the students can be in the sample. Thus, any group of 100 students that contains these two students has no chance of being chosen. Also, students who leave the building late are less likely to be chosen because only the first 500 students leaving have any chance at all of being in the sample. So any group of 100 students that includes a student who is always among the last to leave the building has no chance of being chosen.

    c. Responses may vary. For example, ask every homeroom teacher to have their students fill out a questionnaire.

    d. Yes. Their question could be a source of bias since students are likely to overestimate the amount of homework they do when asked a general question like this. People don't remember exactly how much time they spend on things. The lack of a random sample is another possible source of bias.

    e. Responses may vary. For example, a better procedure would be to have a random sample of students keep track day by day of the amount of homework they do.

 Use after page 134.

Lesson 2 Quiz

1. Jan and Kenyon wanted to organize a picnic for all members of sports teams in their school. They decided to give a survey to members of the sports teams to determine if team members would attend such a picnic. They selected five members from each of the ten sports teams by getting five names from each team's coach. On their survey they asked, "Would you like to attend an all-sports picnic?"

   a. What is the population under investigation in this survey?

   b. Will Jan and Kenyon's procedure for selecting a sample produce a simple random sample?

   c. How could they conduct a census on this question?

   d. Do you think their survey design is biased? Explain your thinking.

   e. Suggest a better procedure.

Unit 2

Lesson 2 Quiz

Suggested Solutions

1. **a.** The population consists of all members of sports teams in Jan and Kenyon's school.

    b. No, this is not a simple random sample, because not every group of 50 sports team members has an equal chance of being selected. For example, using Jan and Kenyon's procedure it would be impossible to select any group of 50 team members that includes more or fewer than five members from any one team. Members of small teams are more likely to be chosen. For example, if Jerry is on a team consisting of six people and Sheila is on a team consisting of 40 people, then for groups with five members from each team, those that contain Jerry are more likely to be chosen than those that contain Sheila. Also, if even one coach gives the survey to the better players (or other favored members), then any group of 50 sports team members that includes the worst players has no chance of being selected.

    c. Responses may vary. For example, ask every coach to have all their team members fill out a questionnaire, with the stipulation that any one person completes just one questionnaire (rather than filling out one for each team that he or she may be on).

    d. Yes. Their question is a source of bias because they are interested in knowing if team members *would* attend and yet they asked if team members *would like* to attend. Thus they are likely to get too many affirmative answers. The question should be reworded to make it more specific. For example: "Would you attend an all-sports picnic on Saturday, October 15, starting at noon, if the cost were $3 per person?" The lack of a random sample is another possible source of bias.

    e. Responses may vary. A better procedure would be to get the list of names of all students on each sports team. If the number were manageable, all students could be contacted. Otherwise, a random sample could be chosen from the list using a table of random numbers. Each person in the sample could be contacted at school or on the telephone.

Use after page 134.

Lesson 3 Quiz

1. According to the *World Almanac and Book of Facts,* about 60% of young adults (age 18–24) live in the home of a parent or guardian or in a college dormitory. (Source: *The World Almanac and Book of Facts 1996.* Mahwah, NJ: World Almanac, 1995.)

    a. Suppose that in a random sample of 40 young adults, there are 18 who live in the home of a parent or guardian or in a college dormitory. Is this result likely or unlikely? Explain.

    b. Describe a way to simulate a random sample of 40 young adults in this situation.

    c. Conduct the simulation you described in Part b and state the sample outcome. Is your sample outcome likely or unlikely? Explain.

Unit 2

Lesson 3 Quiz

2. About 50% of American 14-year-olds are 62 inches tall or less. (Source: *The World Almanac and Book of Facts 1996*. Mahwah, NJ: World Almanac, 1995.)

   a. Suppose you take a random sample of 40 American 14-year-olds and determine the proportion who are 62 inches tall or less. Find the interval that contains all the likely sample proportions. Explain your methods.

   b. In a random sample of 40 American 14-year-olds, 16 were 62 inches tall or less. Is this a likely outcome? Explain.

   c. Suppose you take a random sample of 20 American 14-year-olds and find the proportion who are 62 inches tall or less. Find the interval that contains all of the likely outcomes. Compare it to the interval you found in Part a for a sample of 40. Explain why the intervals compare in size as they do.

Lesson 3 Quiz

Suggested Solutions

Note: Students will need access to the standard 90% box charts, Teaching Masters 55a–55 d, for this quiz.

1. **a.** The result is unlikely, since 18 falls outside the box of likely outcomes for sample size 40 and 60% population percent.

    b. Answers will vary. One way is to enter a command like int(10*rand + 1) on a calculator. Counting 1 through 6 as "yes," press ENTER 40 times and record the number of "yes" outcomes. A table of random digits could also be used.

    c. The sample outcomes will vary. The outcome is likely if it falls between 19 and 29, inclusive. Otherwise it is unlikely.

2. **a.** According to the chart for sample size 40, in 90% of all random samples of size 40, the proportion of 14-year-olds 62 inches tall or less is between 0.375 and 0.625.

    b. 16 is a likely outcome, since it falls between 15 and 25.

    c. According to the chart for sample size 20, in 90% of all random samples of size 20, the proportion of 14-year-olds 62 inches tall or less is between 0.3 and 0.7. The sample size 40 interval width is 0.625 – 0.375 or 0.25 while the sample size 20 width is 0.7 – 0.3 or 0.4. Thus, a larger sample size has a smaller interval width. This is because there is less variability in the sample proportions when the sample size is larger. This is the answer to look for from students. They might elaborate using the Law of Large Numbers. The Law of Large Numbers ensures that the sample proportion will approach 50% (the population proportion) as the size of the sample increases. Thus, this narrowing of the interval for larger sample sizes is to be expected.

Lesson 3 Quiz

1. According to *Pizza Today,* about 50% of American teenagers prefer thin crust pizza to thick crust. (Source: Krantz, Les. *America by the Numbers.* Boston: Houghton Mifflin Company, 1993.)

   a. Suppose that in a random sample of 80 American teenagers there are 45 who prefer thin crust pizza. Is this result likely or unlikely? Explain.

   b. Describe a way to simulate a random sample of 80 teenagers in this situation.

   c. Conduct the simulation you described in Part b and give the sample outcome. Is your sample outcome likely or unlikely? Explain.

 Use after page 152.

Lesson 3 Quiz

2. About 80% of American family vacations are taken in a car rather than by other means of transportation. (Source: Krantz, Les. *America by the Numbers*. Boston: Houghton Mifflin Company, 1993.)

   a. Suppose you take a random sample of 20 American family vacations and determine the proportion of vacations taken by car. Find the interval that contains all the likely sample proportions. Explain your methods.

   b. In a random sample of 20 American family vacations, 10 were by car. Is this a likely outcome? Explain.

   c. Suppose you take a random sample of 40 American family vacations and find the proportion of vacations taken by car. Find the interval of likely sample proportions. Compare it to the interval you found in Part a for a sample of 20. Explain why the intervals compare in size as they do.

Unit 2

Lesson 3 Quiz

Suggested Solutions

Note: Students will need access to the standard 90% box charts, Teaching Masters 55a–55d, for this quiz.

1. **a.** The result is likely, since 45 falls in the box of likely outcomes for sample size 80 and 50% population percent.

    b. Answers will vary. One way is to enter a command like int(10*rand+1) on a calculator. Counting 1 through 5 as "preferring thin crust pizza," press ENTER 80 times and record the number of such outcomes. A table of random digits could also be used.

    c. The sample outcomes will vary. The outcome is likely if it falls between 33 and 47, inclusive. Otherwise, it is unlikely.

2. **a.** According to the chart for sample size 20, in 90% of all random samples of size 20, the proportion of family vacations in which travel is by car is between 0.65 and 0.95.

    b. 10 is not a likely outcome, since it falls below the interval 13 to 19.

    c. According to the chart for sample size 40, in 90% of all random samples of size 40, the proportion of family vacations in which travel is by car is between 0.7 and 0.9. The sample size 20 interval width is 0.95 – 0.65 or 0.3, while the sample size 40 interval width is 0.9 – 0.7 or 0.2. Thus, a larger sample size has a smaller interval width. This is because there is less variability in the sample proportions when the sample size is larger. This is the answer to look for from students. They might elaborate using the Law of Large Numbers. The Law of Large Numbers ensures that the sample proportions will approach 80% (the population proportion) as the size of the sample increases. Thus, this narrowing of the interval for larger sample sizes is to be expected.

Use after page 152.

Lesson 4 Quiz

1. According to a *TV Guide* survey, 65% of adults in a random sample said they watch television while eating. (Source: Krantz, Les. *America by the Numbers*. Boston: Houghton Mifflin Company, 1993.) This survey probably used a large sample, but, to keep things simple, consider only small samples.

   a. If there were 40 people in the sample, what is your estimate of the percentage of all adults who watch television while eating?

   b. What would be your estimate if there were 100 people in the sample?

   c. In the same survey, 40% of adults in the sample said they were offended by too much violence on television. Find a 90% confidence interval for the actual percentage of the adult population that is offended by too much violence on television. Use a sample size of 40.

   d. Find a 90% confidence interval assuming there were only 20 people in the sample.

Lesson 4 Quiz

e. Describe and explain any patterns in this problem between sample size and width of the confidence interval.

2. According to a survey conducted by *Pizza Today*, 46% of American teenagers in a random sample said they prefer thick crust pizza to thin crust. (Source: Krantz, Les. *America by the Numbers.* Boston: Houghton Mifflin Company, 1993.)

a. If the margin of error is 5%, do less than half of all American teenagers prefer thick crust pizza to thin crust? Explain.

b. If the margin of error is 2%, do less than half of all American teenagers prefer thick crust pizza to thin crust? Explain.

Use after page 164.

Lesson 4 Quiz

Suggested Solutions

Note: Students will need access to the standard 90% box charts Teaching Masters 55a–55d for this quiz.

1. Confidence intervals are based on the 90% box charts.

   a. 55%–75%

   b. 60%–70%

   c. 30%–50%

   d. 25%–60%

   e. A larger sample size yields a smaller 90% confidence interval. Since the sample proportion approaches the population proportion as the sample size increases, the 90% box plots get smaller as the sample size increases. In turn, the interval of population percents for which a particular sample proportion is a likely outcome decreases.

2. **a.** Not necessarily. The confidence interval for the percent of American teenagers who prefer thick crust pizza to thin crust is 41%–51%. Since half (50%) is in this interval, we cannot say with confidence that less than half of American teenagers prefer thick crust pizza.

   b. In this case, we can say with confidence that less than half of American teenagers prefer thick crust pizza. The reason is that the confidence interval is now 44%–48% for the percent of American teenagers who prefer thick crust pizza to thin crust, and 50% is outside that interval. (Of course, there is still a chance that the interval 44% – 48% does not contain the actual population percent, so we can't be absolutely certain that less than half of all American teenagers prefer thick crust.)

Unit 2

Lesson 4 Quiz

Form B

1. According to a survey by the National Sporting Goods Association, 25% of adults in a random sample said they bicycle for exercise. (Source: Krantz, Les. *America by the Numbers.* Boston: Houghton Mifflin Company, 1993.) This survey probably used a large sample, but, to keep things simple, consider only small samples.

   a. If there were 40 people in the sample, what is your estimate of the percentage of all adults who bicycle for exercise?

   b. What would be your estimate if there were 100 people in the sample?

   c. In the same survey, 35% of adults in the sample said they swim for exercise. Find a 90% confidence interval for the actual percentage of the adult population that swims for exercise. Use a sample size of 40.

   d. Find a 90% confidence interval assuming there were only 20 people in the sample.

                      Use after page 164.

Unit 2

Lesson 4 Quiz

e. Describe and explain any patterns in this problem between sample size and width of the confidence interval.

2. In the survey described in Activity 1, 35% of adults in the sample said they swim for exercise. (Source: Krantz, Les. *America by the Numbers.* Boston: Houghton Mifflin Company, 1993.)

   a. If the margin of error is 6%, do less than 40% of American adults swim for exercise? Explain.

   b. If the margin of error is 2%, do less than 40% of American adults swim for exercise? Explain.

Unit 2

Lesson 4 Quiz

Form B

Suggested Solutions

Note: Students will need access to the standard 90% box charts, Teaching Masters 55a–55d, for this quiz.

1. Confidence intervals are based on the 90% box charts.

   a. 20%–35%

   b. 20%–30%

   c. 25%–45%

   d. 20%–55%

   e. A larger sample size yields a smaller 90% confidence interval. Since the sample proportion approaches the population proportion as the sample size increases, the 90% box plots get smaller as the sample size increases. In turn, the interval of population percents for which a particular sample proportion is a likely outcome decreases.

2. a. If the margin of error is 6%, the confidence interval for the percent of American adults who swim for exercise is 29%–41%. Since 40% is in this interval, we cannot say with confidence that less than 40% of American adults swim for exercise.

   b. If the margin of error is 2%, the confidence interval for the percent of adults who swim for exercise is 33%–37%. Since 40% is greater than any number in this interval, we can say with confidence that less than 40% of American adults swim for exercise. (Of course, there is still a chance that the interval 33%–37% does not contain the actual population percent, so we can't be absolutely certain that less than 40% of American adults swim for exercise.)

 Use after page 164.

In-Class Exam

1. For an upcoming article in the school paper, the journalism class at Caledonia High School arranged to have all freshmen vote for what they wanted most as a gift. Three favorite gifts, as identified in a national survey, were included on the ballot, and students voted for their first, second, and third preferences. The outcome of the voting is given in the preference table below.

Gift Preference Table

	Rankings			
Clothes	1	2	3	1
Electronic Games	2	1	2	3
Other Games	3	3	1	2
Number of Voters	40	124	180	140

a. Using the plurality method, which gift, if any, is the winner? Explain.

b. Using the runoff method, which gift, if any, is the winner? Explain.

c. Using the pairwise-comparison method, which gift, if any, is the winner? Explain.

Unit 2

In-Class Exam

d. Using the points-for-preferences method, which gift, if any, is the winner? Explain.

e. There can be different winners using different voting methods. What does Arrow's Theorem say about finding a method that always determines a fair winner?

f. A decision often needs to be made based on a vote like the one described in the table. Decide which gift should be called the class favorite in order to best reflect this vote. Write an argument for your choice.

Use after page 168.

In-Class Exam

2. Suppose 70% of parents are planning to give their 12- to 16-year-old children non-electronic games and puzzles, among other things, for the holidays.

   a. The table below shows the results of simulating 60 random samples of 20 parents each and counting the number in each sample who are planning to give their children non-electronic games and puzzles. Construct a 90% box plot for this situation. (Draw your box plot using the axis given below the table. Be sure to label the axis.)

Results of 60 Simulations

Number of Parents Out of 20	Frequency
8	1
9	1
10	2
11	3
12	5
13	7
14	18
15	7
16	10
17	5
18	1

Sample Outcome as a Total

   b. Simulate one more random sample of 20 parents in this situation, and record the number of parents in the sample who are planning to give their children non-electronic games and puzzles for the holidays. Is your result likely or unlikely according to the box plot in Part a? Explain.

In-Class Exam

3. Consider a 90% box plot for samples of size 40. Also consider a 90% confidence interval based on a sample of size 40. Explain how these two differ in meaning and use.

4. Suppose you plan to use a survey to determine how students in your school feel about a possible change in the school dress code. You will need a random sample.

   a. Explain how you could get a simple random sample for your survey.

   b. Describe at least two possible sources of bias that could occur in a survey like this. Explain how you could design your survey to avoid this bias.

Unit 2

In-Class Exam

Suggested Solutions

1. **a.** Clothes and Other Games are tied with 180 first-preference votes each, so there is no plurality winner.

   b. The winner is Clothes over Other Games (304–180).

   c. There is no winner. Electronic Games beats Clothes (304–180), Clothes beats Other Games (304–180), and Other Games beats Electronic Games (320–164).

   d. Assigning 3 points to first preference, 2 to second, and 1 to third gives the following results:

   Clothes: $40(3) + 124(2) + 180(1) + 140(3) = 968$

   Electronic Games: $40(2) + 124(3) + 180(2) + 140(1) = 952$

   Other Games: $40(1) + 124(1) + 180(3) + 140(2) = 984$

   The winner is Other Games with 984 points.

   e. Arrow's Theorem says that, when fairness is defined by Arrow's fairness conditions, there is no voting method that will always determine a fair winner when there are more than two candidates.

   f. Other Games is the most plausible choice since it is the points-for-preferences winner and many experts recommend that method. Students may argue for Clothes, since Clothes is the runoff winner and Clothes tied Other Games using the plurality method. It would be difficult to argue for Electronic Games. Students may argue that there should be no declared favorite because of the conflicting results. Students should defend any answer they give.

2. **a.**

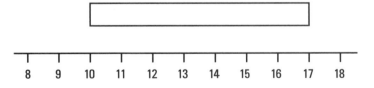

Sample Outcome as a Total

   b. Answers may vary. If a student's simulation result is between 10 and 17 parents who plan to give non-electronic games and puzzles, then the student should say that his or her result is a likely outcome.

Unit 2

Suggested Solutions *(continued)*

3. A 90% box plot is a representation of the distribution of outcomes from all possible samples of size 40 from a given population. The box includes the middle 90% of the sample outcomes, which are defined to be the likely sample outcomes. To determine the 90% box, you must know the population percent. You can use a 90% box to decide if the outcome from a sample of size 40 from a known population is likely, depending on whether the outcome is in the box.

A 90% confidence interval is the interval of population percents for which a given sample outcome is a likely outcome. A confidence interval is used to estimate the unknown population percent based on the outcome from one random sample drawn from the population.

Thus, a 90% box plot is an interval of sample outcomes, based on a known population percent; while a 90% confidence interval is an interval of population percents, used to estimate an unknown population percent.

4. **a.** One way to get a simple random sample is as follows; obtain or create a numbered list of all students in the school. Suppose there are 248 students on the list and you want 50 in your survey. Generate random numbers between 1 and 248, and choose a student corresponding to each random number until you have 50 students.

   b. Some sources of bias that students might identify are poor wording, poor interview methods, poor sample selection, and nonresponse. Students should suggest designing the survey so that the wording is clear and simple; interviews, if used, should be nonthreatening and structured so that interviewees will answer honestly; a random sample should be used; and all efforts should be made to get a high response rate.

In-Class Exam

Form B

1. The senior class officers at Bedford High School decided to have all seniors vote for their favorite weekend activity. Three favorite activities, as identified in several national surveys, were included on the ballot and students voted for their first, second, and third preferences. The outcome of the voting is given in the preference table below.

Weekend Activity Preference Table

	Rankings			
Spectator Outings	1	2	3	1
Boating	2	1	2	3
Pleasure Drives	3	3	1	2
Number of Voters	30	94	120	82

   a. Using the plurality method, which activity, if any, is the winner? Explain.

   b. Using the runoff method, which activity, if any, is the winner? Explain.

   c. Using the pairwise-comparison method, which activity, if any, is the winner? Explain.

Unit 2

In-Class Exam

d. Using the points-for-preferences method, which activity, if any, is the winner? Explain.

e. There can be different winners using different voting methods. What does Arrow's Theorem say about finding a method that always determines a fair winner?

f. A decision often needs to be made based on a vote like the one described in the table. In this case, is there an activity that should be declared the senior class's favorite activity? Write an argument to support your answer.

In-Class Exam

Form B

© 1999 Everyday Learning Corporation

Unit 2

2. Suppose that 40% of American adults often take a drive for pleasure on weekends.

   a. The table below shows the results of simulating 50 random samples of 20 American adults each and recording the number in each sample who often take a drive for pleasure on weekends. Construct a 90% box plot for this situation. (Draw your box plot using the number line given below the table. Be sure to label the number line.)

Results of 50 Simulations

Number Who Drive	Frequency
4	2
5	5
6	8
7	13
8	7
9	6
10	4
11	3
12	2

Sample Outcome as a Total

   b. Simulate one more random sample of 20 American adults in this situation and record the number of American adults in the sample who often take a drive for pleasure on weekends. Is your result likely or unlikely according to the box plot in Part a? Explain.

In-Class Exam

Unit 2

3. In problem A, you want to know whether or not a certain sample outcome is likely. In problem B, you want to estimate the unknown population percent. Explain how to use a 90% box plot or a 90% confidence interval to solve each problem.

4. Suppose you plan to use a survey to determine how students in your school feel about a new four-year mathematics requirement that the school board is considering.

   a. Explain how you could get a random sample for your survey.

   b. Describe at least two possible sources of bias that could occur in a survey like this. Explain how you could design your survey to avoid this bias.

Use after page 168.

In-Class Exam

Suggested Solutions

1. **a.** Pleasure Drives is the plurality winner with 120 first-preference votes.

   b. The winner is Spectator Outings over Pleasure Drives (206–120).

   c. There is no winner. Boating beats Spectator Outings (214–112), Spectator Outings beats Pleasure Drives (206–120), and Pleasure Drives beats Boating (202–124).

   d. Assigning 3 points to first preference, 2 to second, and 1 to third gives the following results:

   Spectator Outings: $30(3) + 94(2) + 120(1) + 82(3) = 644$

   Boating: $30(2) + 94(3) + 120(2) + 82(1) = 664$

   Pleasure Drives: $30(1) + 94(1) + 120(3) + 82(2) = 648$

   The winner is Boating with 664 points.

   e. Arrow's Theorem says that, when fairness is defined by Arrow's fairness conditions, there is no voting method that will always determine a fair winner when there are more than two candidates.

   f. One might plausibly declare Boating to be the favorite activity since Boating is the points-for-preferences winner and many experts recommend that method. However, each activity wins under one of the methods in Parts a–d, so students might argue for any of the activities. They might also reasonably assert that no activity should be declared the class favorite. Students should defend whatever answer they give.

2. **a.**

   Sample Outcome as a Total

   b. Answers may vary. If a student's simulation result is between 5 and 11 inclusive, the student should consider his or her result likely.

Suggested Solutions *(continued)*

3. You can solve problem A using a 90% box plot as follows. Find the standard 90% box plot for samples of the given size from the given population. This box plot is a representation of the distribution of the outcomes from all possible such samples; it spans the middle 90% of all sample outcomes. A sample outcome is defined to be likely if it is in the box.

    You can solve problem B using a 90% confidence interval, as follows. Select a random sample from the population. Compute the sample percent. Then find the interval of population percents for which the sample percent is a likely outcome. This interval is a 90% confidence interval for the actual population percent, and it provides a good estimate for the actual population percent.

4. **a.** One way to get a simple random sample is as follows. Obtain or create a numbered list of all students in the school. Suppose there are 428 students on the list, and you want 80 in your survey. Generate random numbers between 1 and 428, and choose a student corresponding to each random number until you have 80 students.

    b. Some sources of bias that students might identify are poor wording, poor interview methods, poor sample selection, and nonresponse. Students should suggest designing the survey so that the wording is clear and simple; interviews, if used, should be non-threatening and structured so that interviewees will answer honestly; a random sample should be used; and all efforts should be made to get a high response rate.

Take-Home Assessment

1. Suppose that Rob, Lana, Alvin, and Yen Chen are running for class president. Sixty students voted in the election. There is a rule that the winner of the election must receive a majority of the votes. Suppose that Rob received 20 votes, Lana received 17 votes, Alvin received 5 votes, and Yen Chen received 18 votes. What might be done to choose a winner? Defend your answer.

2. Surveying involves a sample of a total population, whereas voting is usually intended to include the entire population. Suppose in an election for a state senate seat, only 30% of the eligible voters actually voted.

   a. In what ways is this like using a survey of the population to determine who wins the senate seat? In what ways is it different?

   b. Since many people do not exercise their right to vote, it has been proposed that a random sample of eligible voters be contacted for their vote and the results used as the official vote. Give arguments for and against the proposal.

3. Percents are involved in different parts of this unit. Explain the following uses of percent: 90% of the voters; 90% of the population has a certain characteristic; 90% box plots; 90% of a random sample has a certain characteristic; 90% confidence interval.

Unit 2

Take-Home Assessment

1. A runoff election seems to make the most sense here. Rob and Yen Chen would be the candidates, since they received the two highest vote totals, although a good argument could be made for including Lana, since she received just one vote fewer than Yen Chen.

2. **a.** This is like using a survey in that only a subset of the population is involved. It is different, however, since the sample of people who vote is not a random sample. The sample of voters is probably not representative of the entire population.

   b. Getting a random sample may be less expensive and simpler than conducting a vote of the entire population. However, people who really were interested in voting would probably be angry if they were not given the opportunity to vote. On the other side of the coin, people who really did not care enough to bother to vote under ordinary circumstances but by chance were included in the random sample, would now cast a (possibly uninformed) vote. There is a good argument for an election being decided by those in the population who are motivated enough to cast a ballot, rather than by a random sample that included many completely apathetic voters.

3. ■ "90% of the voters" refers to 90% of the people who actually cast a vote in an election.

   ■ "90% of the population has a certain characteristic" refers to 90% of all the people under consideration.

   ■ "90% box plots" refers to a box plot of the outcomes from all samples of a specified size in which the interval covered by the "box" contains 90% of the sample outcomes.

   ■ "90% of a random sample has a certain characteristic" refers to 90% of the people chosen to be surveyed from a population.

   ■ "90% confidence interval" refers to the interval of population percents for which a given sample outcome is a likely sample outcome. When this interval is determined using 90% box plots, the interval is called the 90% confidence interval.

  Use after page 168.

Project

The Presidential Election

Purpose

In this unit, you learned about various ways to conduct and evaluate the results of a vote. Initially, this seems like a very simple thing, but that proves not to be the case. For example, Arrow's Theorem shows that, using Arrow's definition of fair, there cannot be a completely fair way to determine a winner if there are more than two candidates. In this project, you will learn about, or review, the method used to elect the president of the United States and explore its history, strengths, and weaknesses.

Directions

The U.S. presidential elections are conducted in two parts, the popular vote and the electoral vote.

■ The popular vote combines all U.S. voters from all states. However, the plurality winner of the popular vote does not necessarily become the President.

■ In the Electoral College vote, each candidate receives all electoral votes of each state in which he or she is the popular vote winner. The losers in the popular vote in a state get none of that state's electoral votes. Different states have different numbers of electoral votes, depending on the number of people who live in the state. For example, California has 52 electoral votes and Montana has just 3.

The person who gets the majority of the electoral votes becomes the President.

1. Explain how a presidential candidate who received a majority of the popular vote in the country in a two-person race could, nevertheless, not be elected President.

2. Do some library research or check with a history teacher to find out if the situation described above in Task 1 has ever happened in a U.S. presidential election. Also, research the historical reasons why this voting system was adopted.

3. Explain how a presidential candidate who finished third in the popular vote in a three-person race could, nevertheless, be elected President.

4. Consider a three-state country in which the states have 5, 3, and 8 electoral votes, respectively. Discuss the possible outcomes of a two-candidate election (both popular vote and Electoral College vote) under the Electoral College method in such a country.

5. Write a report that summarizes your responses to Tasks 1 through 4. Discuss the strengths and weaknesses of the electoral voting method.

Unit 2

Project

The Presidential Election

This project should be done by a pair or group of students in order to encourage discussion and share in the subtasks. An American history teacher would be an especially good resource person for the students.

Suggested Responses

1. A presidential candidate could receive nearly all the popular votes in many states that have few electoral votes and lose by a very small margin in many states that have large numbers of electoral votes.

2. In 1888, although Grover Cleveland had 100,000 more popular votes than Benjamin Harrison, Harrison received the majority of the electoral votes and became president. Twice in history, no candidate has won the majority of the electoral votes, in which case the House of Representatives must decide who will be president. This happened in 1800 when the House elected Thomas Jefferson over Aaron Burr and in 1824 when they elected John Quincy Adams over Andrew Jackson. The main historical reason for the Electoral College method is to prevent states with large populations from always dominating the election process. Large states have more electoral votes than the smaller states, but the margins are much smaller than the population margins.

3. Similar to Task 1 above.

4. Assuming a two-candidate race, the race could be a tie with one candidate winning the electoral votes in the two smaller states. Other combinations would always produce an electoral winner. The popular votes could be in the opposite direction from the electoral votes in the same way as described in Task 1.

5. See Student reports.

Suggested Timeline

Give students a day or two to try the project, then check to see if they are finding appropriate resources for the historical questions. Have them check with you again in a few days, when they believe they have reasonable answers to all the questions and a draft of their paper. The final report should incorporate your feedback to their draft. Depending on how busy your class is with other things, you probably should allow about two weeks for the entire project.

Suggested Evaluation Criteria

1. Format of the report follows directions   10%

2. Accuracy of the responses   60%

3. Quality of writing and clarity of arguments   20%

4. Summary and discussion of electoral college   10%

Project

A Survey of Your Choice

Purpose

In this unit, you learned about surveying, sampling, and some of the probability ideas associated with sampling. To appreciate all this, it will help if you put it together in a real-life survey. In this project, you will do just that; that is, you will choose a survey topic and population and then design, conduct, and report the results of that survey.

Directions

1. Working with a partner or small group, decide on a survey topic that is of interest to you and identify the population in which you want to conduct the survey. There are many ideas for topics in the investigations and MORE tasks in Lessons 2, 3, and 4, but feel free to choose (within reason) whatever topic and accessible population that interests you.

2. Decide on the method by which you will conduct the survey, for example, written, oral in person or by telephone, and so on. Develop the survey instrument using the applicable guidelines for clarity and lack of bias in Lesson 2.

3. Choose a random sample using a method that best fits your survey.

4. Conduct the survey and write a report including a statement of the question you investigated, a description of the population, how you chose a random sample with a justification, and how you administered the survey to the sample. In the results section, include summary statistics, graphs, and any conclusions you can make from your results with the margin of error. (You may want to use the formula for the margin of error on page 161 in your text, rather than relying on the limited box plot charts.) Also describe anything that did not work or that you would change if you were to do the survey over again.

Unit 2

A Survey of Your Choice

This is definitely a group project. Encourage students to choose survey questions that are of particular interest to them. Issues concerning students' most popular musicians, movie stars, sports figures, or presidential candidates often come up, but any reasonable topic that lends itself to a survey will do.

Suggested Timeline

Give students a few days to decide on a topic and population that they want to survey. Discuss it with them, and help them focus on how to choose the sample and conduct the survey. Have them submit a draft of the survey instrument and sampling plan to you for comments before they begin to gather data. Students should be able to complete their survey within a week. It is a good idea to give them a deadline for turning in a draft of their report so you can advise them on it, and then allow them a few more days to revise and turn in the final report.

Suggested Evaluation Criteria

1. Format of the report follows directions	10%
2. Appropriate plan and accurate execution of the sampling	25%
3. Appropriate method of gathering data	25%
4. Accurate and clear presentation of results	25%
5. Appropriate conclusions, margin of error and reflections on method	15%

Lesson 1 Quiz

Form A

1. The following graph shows the time in hours of a 100-mile trip for different average speeds.

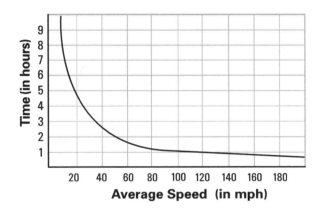

a. Why is it correct to say that *time* is a function of *average speed*?

b. If we use the symbols $y = t(x)$ to represent this function, explain the meaning of y, x, and $y = t(x)$ as they relate to the graph.

c. It is 100 miles from Fort Recovery to Cincinnati. Some friends from Fort Recovery High School decided to drive to Cincinnati to see a Bengals' football game. They averaged 50 mph on their trip to the game. Write the time y in hours of the trip using the $t(x)$ notation and find the actual time in hours. Explain or show your work.

Time in t(x) notation: _____   *Time:* _____

Unit 3

Lesson 1 Quiz

2. The number of chirps made by crickets is a function of the temperature. For a certain species of cricket, the number of chirps per minute is related to the Fahrenheit temperature x with the rule $c(x) = 4x - 148$.

    a. Calculate and explain the meaning of $c(50)$ and $c(78)$.

    $c(50) =$ _____ $c(78) =$ _____

    b. Find the values of x satisfying the equation $c(x) = 92$. What does this mean in terms of the context?

    c. Describe a reasonable practical domain and its corresponding range for the function $c(x)$.

3. For people in your community, is the relation between age in years and hair length a function? Explain why or why not.

Suggested Solutions

1. **a.** There is exactly one value of *time* corresponding to each given value of *average speed.*

    b. *y* is the unique time corresponding to any given value of *x* (average speed). The equation $y = t(x)$ represents this functional relationship between *x* and *y*, so *t* can be thought of as a name for the function.

    c. $t(50)$ is the time that corresponds to an average speed of 50 mph. Referring to the graph, the *y* value corresponding to $x = 50$ is 2. So the time of the trip is 2 hours.

2. **a.** $c(50) = 4(50) - 148 = 52$; $c(78) = 4(78) - 148 = 164$. When the temperature is 50° and 78°, a cricket of this species chirps 52 and 164 times per minute, respectively.

    b. $4x - 148 = 92$, so $x = 60$. A cricket of this species chirps 92 times per minute when the temperature is 60°.

    c. Student choices for an upper limit for temperature may vary based on their experience. The number of chirps *x* must be at least 0. Solving $4x - 148 = 0$ gives $x = 37°$. Choosing a high temperature of 115°, the practical domain is values between 37° and 115°. This function increases. To find the practical range, use $c(37) = 0$ and $c(115) = 312$. The practical range is multiples of 4 in the interval $0 \leq c(x) \leq 312$.

3. There is no unique hair length for each age. For example, two 20-year-olds will probably not have the same hair length.

Unit 3

Lesson 1 Quiz

Form B

1. The following graph shows the height in feet of a Ferris wheel rider for different times (in seconds) after being at the lowest point of the ride.

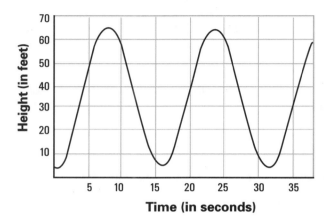

a. Why is it correct to say that *height* is a function of *time*?

b. If we use the symbols $y = h(x)$ to represent this function, explain the meaning of *y, x,* and $y = h(x)$ as they relate to the graph.

c. Andrea was on the ground looking for her friend Emilina, 20 seconds after she saw her in her seat at the bottom of the moving Ferris wheel. Using the $h(x)$ notation, write the height *y* in feet at which Andrea should look for Emilina.

d. Is the time of the ride a function of the height of the Ferris wheel rider? Why or why not?

Lesson 1 Quiz

2. Suppose the income from ticket sales for a concert is related by the function
   $I(x) = -50x^2 + 6,000x$, where x is the price of the ticket.

   a. Calculate and explain the meaning of $I(10)$ and $I(100)$.

   $I(10) =$ _____ $I(100) =$ _____

   b. What values of x satisfy $I(x) = 160,000$? What does this mean in terms of the context?

   c. Describe a reasonable practical domain and its corresponding range for the function $I(x)$.

Unit 3

Suggested Solutions

1. **a.** There is exactly one value of *height* corresponding to each given value of *time*.

   b. y is the unique height corresponding to any given value of x (time). The equation $y = h(x)$ represents this functional relationship between x and y, so h can be thought of as a name for the function.

   c. $h(20)$ is the height that corresponds to a time of 20 seconds. Referring to the graph, the y value corresponding to $x = 20$ appears to be about 39.

   d. No, time is not a function of height because for any one height, you have more than one corresponding time.

2. **a.** $I(10) = \$55,000$ and $I(100) = \$100,000$. When the ticket prices are $10 and $100, the income is $55,000 and $100,000 respectively.

   b. $I(x) = \$160,000$ when $x = 40$ and 80. This means that when ticket price is $40 or $80, income will be $160,000.

   c. One reasonable practical domain would be between $0 and $120, because these values result in a positive income. The corresponding practical range values are values of the function, which are between $0 and $180,000.

Lesson 2 Quiz

1. Suppose you are driving through a state in which there is a 4% sales tax on restaurant meals.

   a. Let p represent the price of a meal. Write a rule giving the cost $C(p)$ of the meal showing the tax added (but not including a tip).

   b. Rewrite your rule in Part a in an equivalent form. Identify the algebraic properties that justify the equivalence of this expression and the one in Part a.

2. For each expression below, find the shortest possible symbolic expression that is equivalent to the one given.

   a. $(2x - 5)(3x)$

   b. $3(m - 2) - 8(2 - 3m)$

   c. $3x - 5x + 9x$

   d. $(4x^3 + 10x^2 + 2x + 7) + (3 + x + 2x^2)$

   e. $-6t^2 - (3t^2 + 5)$

Unit 3

Lesson 2 Quiz

Form A

3. Identify the algebraic properties that justify equivalence of the following pairs of algebraic expressions.

   a. $[-20 + (-3x)] + 5 = [-3x + (-20)] + 5$ by the _____ .

   b. $3y + 4y = (3 + 4)y$ by the _____ .

   c. $6(3 - 4t) = 18 - 24t$ by the _____ .

   d. $(a + 2b) + 3c = a + (2b + 3c)$ by the _____ .

Unit 3

Suggested Solutions

Note: You may wish to have students do this quiz without access to technology.

1. **a.** $C(p) = p + 0.04p$

    b. $C(p) = p(1 + 0.04)$ by the distributive property, and adding gives $C(p) = 1.04p$.

2. **a.** $6x^2 - 15x$

    b. $27m - 22$

    c. $7x$

    d. $4x^3 + 12x^2 + 3x + 10$

    e. $-9t^2 - 5$

3. **a.** Commutative property of addition

    b. Distributive property of multiplication over addition

    c. Distributive property of multiplication over subtraction

    d. Associative property of addition

Unit 3

Lesson 2 Quiz

1. Suppose a department store has a discount of 30% on all summer clothing items.

   a. Let p represent the original price of a summer dress. Write a rule giving the cost $C(p)$ of the dress showing the discount subtracted (but not including tax).

   b. Rewrite your rule in Part a in the shortest equivalent form possible. Identify the algebraic properties that justify the equivalence of this expression and the one in Part a.

2. For each expression below, find the shortest possible symbolic expression that is equivalent to the one given.

   a. $(3x - 4)(5x)$

   b. $5(m - 6) - 6(3 - 5m)$

   c. $8x - 2x + 10x$

   d. $(6y^3 + 4y^2 + 3y) + (y^2 + 2y + 4)$

   e. $-2k^3 - (4 - 6k^3)$

Lesson 2 Quiz

3. Identify the algebraic properties that justify equivalence of the following pairs of algebraic expressions.

   a. $(3x)x^2 = 3(x \cdot x^2)$ by the _____ .

   b. $6 \cdot y \cdot 7 = 6 \cdot 7 \cdot y$ by the _____ .

   c. $-8(x - 4) = -8x + 32$ by the _____ .

   d. $ay + by = (a + b)y$ by the _____ .

Unit 3

Suggested Solutions

Note: You may wish to have students do this quiz without access to technology.

1. **a.** $C(p) = p - 0.3p$

    b. $C(p) = p(1 - 0.3)$ by the distributive property, and subtracting gives $C(p) = 0.7p$.

2. **a.** $15x^2 - 20x$

    b. $35m - 48$

    c. $16x$

    d. $6y^3 + 5y^2 + 5y + 4$

    e. $4k^3 - 4$

3. **a.** Associative property of multiplication

    b. Commutative property of multiplication

    c. Distributive property of multiplication over subtraction

    d. Distributive property of multiplication over addition

Use after page 207.

Unit 3

Lesson 3 Quiz

1. Write each of the following in expanded standard polynomial form.

   a. $(x - 3)(x + 7) =$

   b. $(x + 5)^2 =$

   c. $(2m + 3)(m + 4) =$

   d. $(4 - k)(2k + 5) =$

   e. $(a - 1)^2 =$

2. Rewrite each of the following function rules in an equivalent factored form (where possible).

   a. $f(x) = x^2 - 36$

   b. $g(x) = x^2 + 3x + 3$

   c. $h(t) = t^2 - 10t + 24$

   d. $f(p) = p^2 + 2p + 1$

   e. $g(x) = x^2 + 6x - 16$

   f. $f(x) = 2x^2 + 8x$

Unit 3

Lesson 3 Quiz

3. The sketch below shows some areas that make up a rectangle.

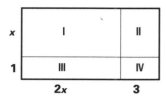

a. Explain why the area of the entire rectangle can be written as $(x + 1)(2x + 3)$.

b. Your explanation in Part a verifies that the area of the entire rectangle is a quadratic function of x given by the rule $A(x) = (x + 1)(2x + 3)$. Find all x in the theoretical domain for which $A(x) = 0$.

c. In this sketch, the entire rectangle is divided into four smaller rectangles marked I, II, III, and IV, respectively. In terms of x, what is the area of each?

Area of I = _____   *Area of II =* _____

Area of III = _____   *Area of IV =* _____

© 1999 Everyday Learning Corporation

Unit 3

Lesson 3 Quiz

d. Show, by algebraic reasoning, that the expression in Part a is equivalent to the sum of the four areas in Part d and to a polynomial in standard form. In other words, start with $(x + 1)(2x + 3)$ and write a sequence of equivalent expressions. At each step, list the property that explains why the new expression is equivalent to the previous one. The last expression must be a polynomial in standard form.

Equivalent expression　　　　　　　　　　　*Reason*

$(x + 1)(2x + 3) =$

4. Write each of these expressions as a single algebraic fraction.

a. $\dfrac{2}{3} + \dfrac{5x}{6} =$

b. $\left(\dfrac{3x^2}{5}\right)\left(\dfrac{11}{x}\right) =$

Unit 3

Suggested Solutions

Note: You may wish to have students do this quiz without access to technology.

1. **a.** $x^2 + 4x - 21$

    b. $x^2 + 10x + 25$

    c. $2m^2 + 11m + 12$

    d. $-2k^2 + 3k + 20$

    e. $a^2 - 2a + 1$

2. **a.** $(x - 6)(x + 6)$

    b. Not factorable

    c. $(t - 6)(t - 4)$

    d. $(p + 1)^2$

    e. $(x + 8)(x - 2)$

    f. $2x(x + 4)$

3. **a.** The area of a rectangle is length times width. Adding the parts of the sides of the rectangle results in $2x + 3$ for the length and $x + 1$ for the width, so the area is $(2x + 3)(x + 1)$ or $(x + 1)(2x + 3)$.

    b. To find x for which $A(x) = 0$, set each factor equal to 0. $x + 1 = 0$ gives $x = -1$, and $2x + 3 = 0$ gives $x = -\frac{3}{2}$.

    c. Area of I $= 2x^2$ Area of II $= 3x$
        Area of III $= 2x$ Area of IV $= 3$

    d. Some of the following steps may be combined in your students' work. Give credit if the sequence and reasons are correct, even if some of the detail is missing.

$(x + 1)(2x + 3) = (x + 1)(2x) + (x + 1)(3)$	Distributive property
$= (2x^2 + 2x) + (3x + 3)$	Distributive property
$= 2x^2 + (2x + 3x) + 3$	Associative property
$= 2x^2 + (2 + 3)x + 3$	Distributive property
$= 2x^2 + 5x + 3$	Arithmetic

4. **a.** $\dfrac{2}{3} + \dfrac{5x}{6} = \dfrac{4}{6} + \dfrac{5x}{6} = \dfrac{4 + 5x}{6}$

    b. $\left(\dfrac{3x^2}{5}\right)\left(\dfrac{11}{x}\right) = \left(\dfrac{33x^2}{5x}\right) = \left(\dfrac{33x}{5x}\right)$

Use after page 224.

Lesson 3 Quiz

1. Write each of the following in expanded standard polynomial form.

   a. $(r - 5)(r + 5) =$

   b. $(y - 2)(2y + 1) =$

   c. $(x - 1)^2 =$

   d. $(y + 3)^2 =$

   e. $(5 - x)(2x + 1) =$

2. Rewrite each of the following function rules in an equivalent factored form (where possible).

   a. $f(x) = x^2 - x - 12$

   b. $g(x) = x^2 - 49$

   c. $h(t) = t^2 - 4t + 5$

   d. $f(p) = p^2 + 8p + 16$

   e. $g(x) = x^2 + 7x - 18$

   f. $f(x) = 6x - 18x$

Unit 3

Lesson 3 Quiz

3. The sketch below shows some areas that make up a rectangle.

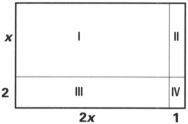

a. Explain why the area of the entire rectangle can be written as $(x + 2)(2x + 1)$.

b. Your explanation in Part a verifies that the area of the entire rectangle is a quadratic function of x given by the rule $A(x) = (x + 2)(2x + 1)$. Find all x in the theoretical domain for which $A(x) = 0$.

c. In this sketch, the entire rectangle is divided into four smaller rectangles marked I, II, III, and IV, respectively. In terms of x, what is the area of each?

Area of I = _____   *Area of II* = _____

Area of III = _____   *Area of IV* = _____

Lesson 3 Quiz

Form B

d. Show, by algebraic reasoning, that the expression in Part a is equivalent to the sum of the four areas in Part d and to a polynomial in standard form. In other words, start with $(x + 2)(2x + 1)$ and write a sequence of equivalent expressions. At each step, list the property that explains why the new expression is equivalent to the previous one. The last expression must be a polynomial in standard form.

Equivalent expression   *Reason*

$(x + 2)(2x + 1) =$

4. Write each of these expressions as a single algebraic fraction.

a. $\dfrac{5}{9} + \dfrac{3x}{4} =$

b. $\left(\dfrac{p}{3}\right) \cdot \left(\dfrac{15}{p^2}\right) =$

Unit 3

Suggested Solutions

Note: You may wish to have students do this quiz without access to technology.

1. **a.** $r^2 - 25$

    b. $2y^2 - 3y - 2$

    c. $x^2 - 2x + 1$

    d. $y^2 + 6y + 9$

    e. $-2x^2 + 9x + 5$

2. **a.** $(x - 4)(x + 3)$

    b. $(x - 7)(x + 7)$

    c. Not factorable

    d. $(p + 4)^2$

    e. $(x + 9)(x - 2)$

    f. $6x(x - 3)$

3. **a.** The area of a rectangle is length times width. Adding the parts of the sides of the rectangle results in $2x + 1$ for the length and $x + 2$ for the width, so the area is $(2x + 1)(x + 2)$.

    b. To find x for which $A(x) = 0$, set each factor equal to 0. $2x + 1 = 0$ gives $x = -\frac{1}{2}$, and $x + 2 = 0$ gives $x = -2$.

    c. Area of I $= 2x^2$ Area of II $= x$
    Area of III $= 4x$ Area of IV $= 2$

    d. Some of the following steps may be combined in your students' work. Give credit if the sequence and reasons are correct, even if some of the detail is missing.

    $$
    \begin{aligned}
    (x + 2)(2x + 1) &= (x + 2)(2x) + (x + 2)(1) && \text{Distributive property} \\
    &= (2x^2 + 4x) + (x + 2) && \text{Distributive property} \\
    &= 2x^2 + (4x + x) + 2 && \text{Associative property} \\
    &= 2x^2 + (4 + 1)x + 2 && \text{Distributive property} \\
    &= 2x^2 + 5x + 2 && \text{Arithmetic}
    \end{aligned}
    $$

4. **a.** $\dfrac{5}{9} + \dfrac{3x}{4} = \dfrac{20}{36} + \dfrac{27x}{36} = \dfrac{20 + 27x}{36}$

    b. $\left(\dfrac{p}{3}\right) \cdot \left(\dfrac{15}{p^2}\right) = \dfrac{15p}{3p^2} = \dfrac{5}{p}$

Lesson 4 Quiz

1. For the summer following his junior year, Hakeem applied at several restaurants for jobs as a waiter. Season's Finest and The Provincial Room both offered him jobs. In both cases, Hakeem's weekly pay would depend on a base salary and the amount in dollars x of the sales at the tables he served. For a normal work week at Season's Finest, Hakeem would earn $0.15x + 40$ dollars. At The Provincial Room, he would earn $0.1x + 50$ dollars.

   a. What do the numbers 0.15, 40, 0.1, and 50 in the two rules tell about how Hakeem's pay would be calculated?

   Write and solve (without calculator tables or graphs) equations and inequalities to answer the following questions. Include all steps in your reasoning.

   b. For what dollar value of sales would Hakeem's pay at the two restaurants be equal?

   c. For what dollar value of sales would his pay at Season's Finest be greater than that at The Provincial Room?

Unit 3

d. What dollar value of sales would be required at Season's Finest for Hakeem to earn more than $100?

e. Hakeem accepted the offer at The Provincial Room. If he earned $170 for his first full week, what was the dollar value of sales at his tables?

2. Use what you have learned about the quadratic formula to solve the following problems. Show your work in each case.

a. Find the zeros and the minimum value of $f(x) = x^2 + 4x - 8$.

b. Graph solutions for $x^2 - x - 12 \le 0$.

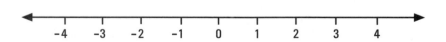

Unit 3

Suggested Solutions

Note: You may wish to have students do this quiz without access to technology. Task 2 may then be left in radical (square root) form.

1. **a.** The numbers 40 and 50 are the base salaries at Season's Finest and The Provincial Room, respectively. The numbers 0.15 and 0.1 are the ratios of the sales, probably in the form of tips, that Hakeem would receive if he worked at the respective restaurants.

    b. $0.15x + 40 = 0.1x + 50$
    $$0.05x = 10$$
    $$x = 200$$
    For sales of $200, Hakeem's earnings at the two restaurants would be equal.

    c. $0.15x + 40 > 0.1x + 50$
    $$0.05x > 10$$
    $$x > 200$$
    For sales greater than $200, his wages would be greater at Season's Finest.

    d. $0.15x + 40 > 100$
    $$0.15x > 60$$
    $$x > 400$$
    For sales greater than $400, Hakeem would earn more than $100 dollars at Season's Finest.

    e. $0.1x + 50 = 170$
    $$0.1x = 120$$
    $$x = 1,200$$
    Sales at Hakeem's tables were $1,200.

2. **a.** The zeros are $x = -\dfrac{4}{2} \pm \dfrac{\sqrt{48}}{2} \approx -2 \pm 3.46$, or $x \approx 1.46$ and $x \approx -5.46$.
    The minimum value is -12 when $x = -2$.

    b. $(x - 4)(x + 3) \leq 0$ for $-3 \leq x \leq 4$

Unit 3

Lesson 4 Quiz

1. Two taxicab companies in Central City, Green Cab and Blue Cab, use different formulas to compute their fares. In both cases, the fares in dollars depend on a minimum charge plus an amount per mile driven. Green Cab's formula for fares is $3.5x + 4$ and Blue Cab's is $2.5x + 6.5$, where x represents the number of miles driven.

   a. What do the numbers 3.5, 4, 2.5, and 6.5 in the two formulas tell about how each company calculates fares?

   Write and solve (without calculator tables or graphs) equations and inequalities to answer the following questions. Include all steps in your reasoning.

   b. For what length trip would the two companies' fares be equal?

   c. For what length trip would Green Cab's fares be greater than Blue Cab's?

Unit 3

Lesson 4 Quiz

d. How long must a trip be for the Green Cab fare to be more than $25?

e. If you paid $11 for a trip to your grandmother's house in a Blue Cab, how long was your trip?

2. Use what you have learned about the quadratic formula to solve the following problems. Show your work in each case.

   a. Find the zeros and the minimum value of $f(x) = x^2 + 2x - 2$.

   b. Graph solutions for $x^2 + 2x - 8 \leq 0$.

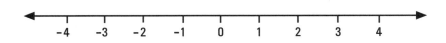

© 1999 Everyday Learning Corporation

Unit 3

Suggested Solutions

Note: You may wish to have students do this quiz without access to technology. Task 2 may then be left in radical (square root) form.

1. **a.** The numbers 4 and 6.5 (or $4 and $6.50) are the minimum charges per trip by Green Cab and Blue Cab, respectively. The numbers 3.5 and 2.5 (or $3.50 and $2.50) are the rates per mile charged by the respective cab companies.

   b. $3.5x + 4 = 2.5x + 6.5$
   $$x = 2.5$$
   For a trip of 2.5 miles, the fares of the two cab companies would be equal.

   c. $3.5x + 4 > 2.5x + 6.5$
   $$x > 2.5$$
   For a trip longer than 2.5 miles, Green Cab's fare would be greater.

   d. $3.5x + 4 > 25$
   $$3.5x > 21$$
   $$x > 6$$
   For trips longer than 6 miles, Green Cab's fare would be greater than $25.

   e. $2.5x + 6.5 = 11$
   $$2.5x = 4.5$$
   $$x = 1.8 \text{ miles}$$
   Your trip was 1.8 miles.

2. **a.** The zeros are $x = \frac{-2}{2} \pm \frac{\sqrt{12}}{2} \approx -1 \pm \sqrt{3} \approx -1 \pm 1.73$, or $x \approx 0.73$ and $x \approx -2.73$. The minimum value is -3 when $x = -1$.

   b. $(x + 4)(x - 2) \leq 0$ for $-4 \leq x \leq 2$

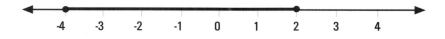

Use after page 239.

© 1999 Everyday Learning Corporation

Unit 3

Lesson 5 Quiz

1. A teacher in New Mexico uses the following number trick to amaze her students. She directs each student to pick a number between 0 and 10 and to do the following calculations:

   Add 3 to the number.

   Then multiply the result by 4.

   Then divide the result by 2.

   Then subtract 6 from that result.

   Prove that whatever the starting number, these calculations will always bring you back to that number times 2.

2. Use algebraic reasoning to find formulas for solving any equation of the following types for x in terms of a, b, and c. Provide justification for each step in your reasoning.

   a. $a(x + b) = c$

   b. $\dfrac{a}{x} = b + 1$

Unit 3

3. Quadrilateral *ABCD* sketched below is an isosceles trapezoid. Prove that the lengths of diagonals *AC* and *BD* are equal.

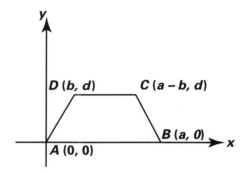

© 1999 Everyday Learning Corporation

Suggested Solutions

1. Call the number you choose x and follow the steps in the calculations.

Add 3 to the number:	$x + 3$
Then multiply the result by 4:	$4(x + 3)$
Then divide the result by 2:	$2(x + 3) = 2x + 6$
Then subtract 6 from that result:	$2x + 6 - 6 = 2x$

2. **a.** $a(x + b) = c$ is given.

Divide both sides by a:	$x + b = \dfrac{c}{a}$.
Subtract b from both sides:	$x = \dfrac{c}{a} - b$.

   b. $\dfrac{a}{x} = b + 1$ is given. (Note that $x \neq 0$.)

Multiply both sides by x:	$a = x(b + 1)$.
Divide both sides by $b + 1$:	$x = \dfrac{a}{b + 1}$.

3. Use the distance formula:
$$AC = \sqrt{(a - b - 0)^2 + (d - 0)^2} = \sqrt{(a - b)^2 + d^2} = BD$$

Unit 3

Lesson 5 Quiz

1. A teacher in Maine uses the following number trick to amaze his students. He directs each student to pick a number between 0 and 10 and to do the following calculations:

   Multiply the number by 2.
   Then add 4 to the result.
   Then divide the result by 2.
   Then subtract 2 from that result.

   Prove that whatever the starting number, these calculations will always bring you back to that number.

2. Use algebraic reasoning to find formulas for solving any equation of the following types for x in terms of a, b, and c. Provide justification for each step in your reasoning.

   a. $a(x - b) = c$

   b. $\dfrac{a}{x} - b = 1$

Use after page 252.

Unit 3

3. Quadrilateral *ABCD* sketched below is an isosceles trapezoid. Prove or disprove that the diagonals *AC* and *BD* bisect each other.

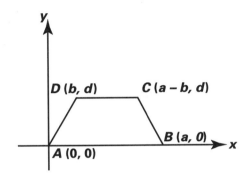

Unit 3

Suggested Solutions

1. Call the number you choose x and follow the steps in the calculations.

   Multiply the number by 2: $2x$

   Then add 4 to the result: $2x + 4$

   Then divide the result by 2: $\dfrac{2(x+2)}{2} = x + 2$

   Then subtract 2 from that result: $x + 2 - 2 = x$

2. **a.** $a(x - b) = c$ is given.

   Divide both sides by a: $x - b = \dfrac{c}{a}$.

   Add b to both sides: $x = \dfrac{c}{a} + b$.

   b. $\dfrac{a}{x} - b = 1$ is given.

   Add b to both sides: $\dfrac{a}{x} = 1 + b$.

   Multiply both sides by x: $a = x(1 + b)$.

   Divide both sides by $1 + b$ (or $b + 1$): $x = \dfrac{a}{b+1}$.

3. Find the midpoint of AC: $\left(\dfrac{a-b}{2}, \dfrac{d}{2}\right)$.

   Find the midpoint of BD: $\left(\dfrac{a+b}{2}, \dfrac{d}{2}\right)$.

   The midpoints are not the same, so the statement is disproved.

Unit 3

In-Class Exam

1. The fuel economy in miles per gallon of a car's engine is a function of the speed x in miles per hour that the car is driven. Based on experimental data, one auto company found that this function for its best selling car is $f(x) = -0.01x^2 + 1.2x - 5.8$.

   a. Calculate and explain the meaning of $f(50)$.

   b. Describe a reasonable practical domain and range for the function $f(x)$. Explain.

   c. Describe the theoretical domain and range for the function $f(x)$. Explain.

   d. Use the quadratic formula to find the zeroes and the line of symmetry of the function $f(x)$. Keeping in mind that this function is an estimate based on experimental data, explain what the zeroes tell about the fuel economy and the speed of the car.

   e. Find the maximum value of the function $f(x)$. Explain what this tells about the fuel economy and the speed of the car.

Unit 3

In-Class Exam

f. The speed limit on Interstate 80 was recently increased from 55 to 65 miles per hour in the vicinity of the Quad Cities. If this car is driven at the speed limit, describe the effect of the change of the speed limit on the car's fuel economy.

2. Rewrite the following expressions or functions in standard polynomial form.

    a. $(2x^3 - 4x) - 3(4x^3 - x^2 + 5x - 9)$

    b. $(y + 7)^2$

    c. $f(x) = (x + 3)(x - 7)$

    d. $g(x) = (6 - 3x)(4x) - 2(7 - x)$

    e. $(x - 3)(4x + 1)$

3. Solve the equation $x^2 + 9x + 18 = 0$ using one method that does not require a calculator and one method which uses the calculator. Explain your methods.

© 1999 Everyday Learning Corporation

Unit 3

In-Class Exam

4. Graph the solutions for the following inequalities and explain your methods.

   a. $x^2 - 7x + 12 < 0$

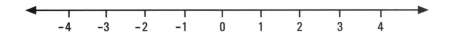

   b. $3x - 4 > 6x + 5$

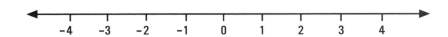

5. In a science class, the teacher had given three exams and graded each on a scale from 0 to 20. For official records, the teacher needed to convert those scores to a scale from 0 to 100 and decided to multiply each exam score by 5. Suppose a student had scores of x, y, and z on the 0 to 20 scale.

   a. Using original grades on the scale from 0 to 20, what formula will give the student's average?

   b. What formula will give the student's average when the new scale is used?

   c. Is it true that the student's average on the 0 to 100 scale will simply be 5 times the average on the 0 to 20 scale? Use algebraic reasoning to prove or disprove this conjecture.

Unit 3

In-Class Exam

6. Quadratic functions, with graphs that are parabolas, can be written in the standard polynomial form $f(x) = ax^2 + bx + c$ or in factored form.

    a. What information about the function can you determine by examining the standard polynomial form?

    b. What information about the function can you determine by examining the factored form?

    c. If p and q are the zeroes of a quadratic function, what do you know about the graph of the function? The line of symmetry of the function?

© 1999 Everyday Learning Corporation

Unit 3

Suggested Solutions

1. **a.** $f(50) = -0.01(50)^2 + 1.2(50) - 5.8 = 29.2$;
   At 50 miles per hour, the fuel economy is 29.2 miles per gallon.

   b. A reasonable practical domain is about 0 to 100 miles per hour. The practical range values are function values between 0 and 30.2 miles per gallon.

   c. The theoretical domain is all real numbers.
   The theoretical range is all numbers less than or equal to 30.2.

   d. The zeroes are about 5.05 and 114.95. Halfway between these two values, the line of symmetry has the equation $x = 60$. Ordinarily, the zeroes would be the speed at which the car gets 0 miles per gallon. In fact, these values are estimates. In reality, $x = 0$ would be one zero and the other would occur at a point beyond the maximum speed of the car.

   e. The maximum value will occur on the line of symmetry, $x = 60$. The fuel economy at that point is $f(60) = 30.2$ miles per gallon.

   f. The fuel economy is unchanged since it is the same (29.95 miles per gallon) at 55 as it is at 65 miles per hour.

2. **a.** $-10x^3 + 3x^2 - 19x + 27$

   b. $y^2 + 14y + 49$

   c. $f(x) = x^2 - 4x - 21$

   d. $g(x) = -12x^2 + 26x - 14$

   c. $4x^2 - 11x - 3$

3. Methods will vary. Following are some possibilities.

   - Factor, set each factor equal to 0, and solve.
   - Graph $y = x^2 + 9x + 18$ and note that the solutions are the x-intercepts.
   - Use the same equation as above and the table feature on a graphics calculator; then scroll to find the values of x that correspond to $y = 0$.
   - Use the quadratic formula.
   - Use the solve capability of a calculator.

   In any case, the solutions are $x = -3$ and $x = -6$.

Unit 3

Suggested Solutions *(continued)*

4. **a.** Students may factor, use the quadratic formula, the solve capability, tables, or graphs to determine that the roots are 3 and 4. The solution to the inequality is $3 < x < 4$.

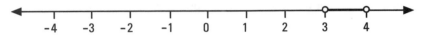

    b. $x < -3$

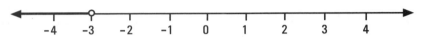

5. **a.** The average on a scale of 0 to 20 is $\frac{1}{3}(x + y + z)$ or $\left(\frac{x+y+z}{3}\right)$.

    b. The average on a scale of 0 to 100 is $\frac{1}{3}(5x + 5y + 5z)$ or $\left(\frac{5x+5y+5z}{3}\right)$.

    c.
$$\frac{5x + 5y + 5z}{3} = \frac{5(x + y + z)}{3}$$
$$= \frac{5}{1} \cdot \frac{x + y + z}{3}$$
Thus, $\dfrac{5x + 5y + 5z}{3} = 5 \cdot \dfrac{x + y + z}{3}$

This means that 5 times the average on the 0 to 20 scale is the same as the average on the 0 to 100 scale.

6. **a.** You can tell if the function has a maximum value (if $a < 0$) or minimum value (if $a > 0$) and that the y-intercept is c.

    b. From the factored form, you can easily determine the zeroes of the function.

    c. The graph of the function crosses the x-axis at p and at q. The line of symmetry is $y = \frac{p+q}{2}$.

Unit 3

In-Class Exam

Form B

1. Based on data from similar concerts in the past, the predicted profit as a function of x, the price per ticket in dollars, for an upcoming band concert is $P(x) = -50x^2 + 4{,}000x - 7{,}500$.

   a. Calculate and explain the meaning of $P(25)$.

   b. Describe a reasonable practical domain and range for the function $P(x)$. Explain.

   c. Describe the theoretical domain and range for the function $P(x)$. Explain.

   d. Use the quadratic formula to find the zeroes and the line of symmetry of the function $P(x)$. Keeping in mind that this function is an estimate based on similar past data, explain what the zeroes tell about the profit and the price of a ticket.

   e. Use the quadratic formula to help find the maximum value of the function $P(x)$. Explain what this tells about the profit and the price of a ticket.

Unit 3

In-Class Exam

f. The concert promoter was planning to charge $30 per ticket, but at the last minute she increased the price to $50. Describe the effect of this change in ticket price on predicted profit.

2. Rewrite the following expressions or functions in standard polynomial form.

a. $(x^3 - 4x + 8) - 2(3x^3 + 2x^2 - 5x)$

b. $(2x + 3)^2$

c. $f(x) = (2x - 1)(x^3 + 4x)$

d. $(5 + 8x)(2x) - 3(4 - 2x)$

e. $(3x - 2)(6x - 8)$

3. Solve the equation $x^2 - 9x + 20 = 0$ using one method that does not require a calculator and one method that uses the calculator. Explain your methods.

In-Class Exam

4. Graph the solutions for the following inequalities and explain your methods.

   a. $x^2 + x - 12 < 0$

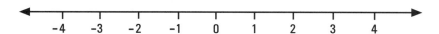

   b. $5x - 4 > -2x + 10$

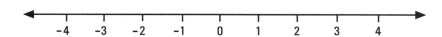

5. Use algebraic reasoning to find a formula for solving any equation of the type $(a + b)x = c(x + d)$. Provide justification for each step in your reasoning.

Unit 3

In-Class Exam

6. Quadratic functions, with graphs that are parabolas, can be written in the standard polynomial form, $f(x) = ax^2 + bx + c$, or in factored form.

   a. What information about the function can you determine by examining the standard polynomial form?

   b. What information about the function can you determine by examining the factored form?

   c. If p and q are the zeroes of a quadratic function, what do you know about the graph of the function? The line of symmetry of the function?

Suggested Solutions

1. **a.** $P(25) = -50(25)^2 + 4,000(25) - 7,500 = 61,250$
   The predicted profit if tickets are priced at $25 is $61,250.

   b. A reasonable practical domain is about $20 to $60, depending on how much the local audiences will be willing to pay to attend the concert. For this practical domain, the range is $52,500 to $72,500.

   c. The theoretical domain is all real numbers.
   The theoretical range is all numbers less than or equal to 72,500.

   d. The zeroes are approximately 1.92 and 78.08. The line of symmetry which is halfway between these two values has equation $x = 40$. The zeroes would be the price of a ticket for which no profit would be expected.

   e. The maximum value will occur on the line of symmetry, $x = 40$. The predicted profit at that point is $P(40) = \$72,500$. Thus, the maximum profit of $72,500 would be obtained if the ticket price were $40.

   f. The predicted profit would remain unchanged since $P(30) = P(50) = \$67,500$.

2. **a.** $-5x^3 - 4x^2 + 6x + 8$

   b. $4x^2 + 12x + 9$

   c. $f(x) = 2x^4 - x^3 + 8x^2 - 4x$

   d. $16x^2 + 16x - 12$

   e. $18x^2 - 36x + 16$

3. Methods will vary. Following are some possibilities.

   ▪ Factor, set each factor equal to 0, and solve.
   ▪ Graph $y = x^2 - 9x + 20$ and note that the solutions are the x-intercepts.
   ▪ Use the same equation as above and the table feature on a graphics calculator, then scroll to find the values of x that correspond to $y = 0$.
   ▪ Use the quadratic formula.
   ▪ Use the solve capability of a calculator.

   In any case, the solutions are $x = 4$ and $x = 5$.

Unit 3

In-Class Exam

Form B

Suggested Solutions *(continued)*

4. **a.** Students may factor, use the quadratic formula, the solve capability, tables, or graphs to determine that the roots are -4 and 3. The solution to the inequality is $-4 < x < 3$.

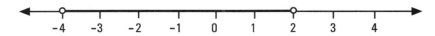

   b. $x > 2$

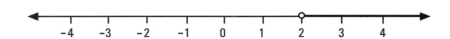

5. $(a + b)x = c(x + d)$ is given.
    Use the distributive property on both sides: $ax + bx = cx + cd$.
    Subtract cx from both sides: $ax - bx - cx = cd$.
    Factor the left side: $(a - b - c)x = cd$.
    Divide both sides by $a - b - c$: $x = \dfrac{cd}{a - b - c}$.

6. **a.** You can tell if the function has a maximum value (if $a < 0$) or minimum value (if $a > 0$) and that the y-intercept is c.

   b. From the factored form, you can easily determine the zeroes of the function.

   c. The graph of the function crosses the x-axis at p and at q. The line of symmetry is $y = \dfrac{p + q}{2}$.

Take-Home Assessment

1. Write a test that you think would adequately cover all of the important ideas in this unit. The test should be written at a level of difficulty that is appropriate for your classmates. Use the "Checkpoint" and "On Your Own" features as a guide. Your test should reflect the expectations for student learning in this unit. Provide an answer key and a guide for scoring your test.

2. In this unit, you learned about factoring expressions like $2x^2 - x - 1$.

   a. Find the factors of this expression.

   b. Graph the function $y = 2x^2 - x - 1$ with your calculator.

   c. Is there any connection between the graph in Part a and the factors? Explain.

   d. Use a graph and the connection that you saw in Part c to find factors of $2x^3 + 5x^2 - x - 6$.

   e. Describe in your own words how to find factors of an algebraic expression $f(x)$ (for example, of the two expressions above), using the graph of $y = f(x)$.

3. The graph of a certain quadratic function crosses the x-axis only at $x = -4$ and $x = 3$.

   a. Sketch an example of such a graph. Explain.

   b. Sketch the graphs of two more quadratic functions that cross the x-axis at the given points. Explain.

   c. Write an equation of the function that corresponds to the quadratic function with a y-intercept of 8 and zeroes of -4 and 3. Explain your work.

   d. Give as complete a description as you can of the equation of any quadratic function whose graph crosses the x-axis only at $x = -4$ and $x = 3$.

Unit 3

1. This project can be done by a student working alone or by pairs of students. The students' choices of test items will be a good indication of what they think is important. Be flexible in your grading of this project. Base grades on the consistency of what the students choose to do, the accuracy of solutions, and the completeness of coverage of the test. If time permits, it would be interesting to have other students complete a test constructed by classmates, followed by a class discussion of the test.

2. **a.** $(2x + 1)(x - 1)$

   b.

   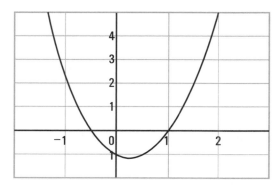

   c. The x-intercepts, -0.5 and 1, are the solutions of the equations obtained by setting each factor equal to 0, that is, $2x + 1 = 0$ and $x - 1 = 0$.

   d. First, graph $y = 2x^3 + 5x^2 - x - 6$.

   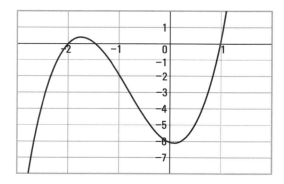

   Note that the x-intercepts are -2, -1.5, and 1. These are solutions of $x + 2 = 0$, $x + 1.5 = 0$, and $x - 1 = 0$, respectively. The second equation, $x + 1.5 = 0$, can be rewritten with whole number coefficients by multiplying both sides by 2, giving $2x + 3 = 0$. Multiplying the left-hand expressions gives $y = (x + 2)(2x + 3)(x - 1)$. Students should check that this is indeed equivalent to $2x^3 + 5x^2 - x - 6$.

   e. In general, if the x-intercepts of the graph of polynomial $f(x)$ are, for example, a, b, and c, then the factors of $f(x)$ are $k(x - a)(x - b)(x - c)$, where k is any nonzero number. This approach also works if there are four or more x-intercepts.

Unit 3

3. **a.** Any parabola with *x*-intercepts −4 and 3 works, for example:

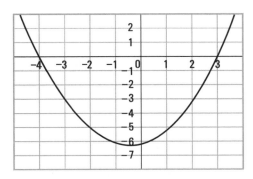

b. Two possible graphs are shown below.
Sample:

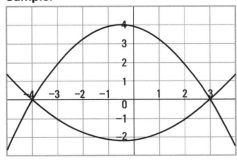

c. $y = -\frac{2}{3}(x + 4)(x - 3) = -\frac{2}{3}x^2 - \frac{2}{3}x + 8$

d. Any quadratic function whose factored form is $y = k(x + 4)(x - 3)$, where *k* is any nonzero number, will suffice.

Unit 3

Project

Algebra II and You

Purpose

The mathematics in this curriculum is not organized into separate algebra and geometry courses like many high school mathematics programs are. The purpose of this project is to have you compare some of your mathematical experience to a typical Algebra II approach. You will find that you have learned most of the topics in these courses, but with a different emphasis. In addition, you have experience with a much broader array of mathematical models and methods.

Directions

1. Get an Algebra II (or advanced algebra) textbook from your teacher.

2. Skim through the book. Look at the titles of chapters and sections. Make a list of the topics that you have not seen before. Some, but not all, of the topics on your list will be included in later units of this curriculum.

3. Go back over Units 1 and 3 of this course and make a similar list of topics that are included in this course but not in the Algebra II book. Some of the topics on your list are in a geometry course rather than in an algebra course. Many other topics on the list are not included in those high school mathematics curricula that are organized around geometry and algebra topics.

4. Choose two chapters in the Algebra II book that seem to be most like the content of Units 1 and 3. For example, there are probably chapters on quadratic equations, powers and roots, and maybe on functions. Examine these two chapters in more detail. Compare how topics in the *Contemporary Mathematics in Context* units are treated in the Algebra II book. Also, examine the end-of-chapter exercises in these Algebra II chapters and compare them to the MORE tasks in this unit.

5. Write a report that includes (a) the title, author, and publisher of the Algebra II book you looked at, (b) an introduction that describes exactly what comparisons you made and how you made them, (c) the lists of topics described in Parts 2 and 3 above with a written comparison of the two lists and what they mean, (d) a description of what you found in the two chapters you examined and how it compared to *Contemporary Mathematics in Context*, and finally (e) a short closing in which you describe in your own words the most important differences between what you are doing in this course and what is in the Algebra II book.

Algebra II and You

This project can probably be done best by a small group of students, since they can divide the task of reviewing the Algebra II book. You may want to choose chapters from the Algebra II book rather than have the students choose their own. The purpose is for them to see that they are learning many of the ideas in Algebra II, as well as many others, in probability, statistics, and discrete mathematics. They should also note the modeling approach, which is an attempt to make the mathematics useful and meaningful in *CMIC* compared to the approach through a sequence of algebraic skills in the Algebra II book. At this point, *CMIC* students will not have any experience simplifying complex rational expressions, a topic in most Algebra II books. Most other Algebra II topics have already been included in *CMIC* or will be in future units. It should be very interesting to see on which differences in approach the students focus. More use of the calculator, more modeling and applications, and more group discussions and problem solving are likely to be cited, while there is less practice, fewer short out-of-context exercises, and fewer worked examples. The MORE tasks tend to be much longer, more applied, and more exploratory than the shorter, single-method, single-answer exercises in most Algebra II books.

Suggested Timelines

Give students a day or two to work on the project; then check to see if they understand what needs to be done. Check whether they have chosen appropriate topics and are making good judgments about differences. Also verify that they have chosen two chapters that significantly overlap the content of this unit. Have students submit a rough draft of the report. If it shows major misconceptions or requires editing, return it with your feedback and give them a second deadline for submitting the report in its final form. Students should have from several days to a week to submit the first draft and, if necessary, a few more days for the final report.

Suggested Evaluation Criteria

1. Format of the report follows directions   10%
2. Accuracy and completeness of the introduction   15%
3. Accuracy of the lists of topics and explanations   30%
4. Accurate and clear comparison of two chapters   30%
5. Clear and accurate summary of differences   15%

Unit 3

Project

Multiple Algebraic Methods

Purpose

In this unit, you learned several procedures for solving equations and inequalities and for finding algebraic expressions that are equivalent to ones that are given. To make these procedures work for you, it is important that you understand what a procedure is accomplishing, how to carry it out with paper and pencil or calculator as appropriate, and how to check it for accuracy. In this project, you will pull these solution and checking methods together for a variety of expressions from the unit.

Directions

1. Following are exercises for solving or simplifying equations or inequalities like those you did in this unit. For each exercise:

    ■ Solve it with paper and pencil.

    ■ Solve it by using your calculator.

    ■ Check your solution using paper and pencil.

    ■ Check your solution using your calculator.

    Show and explain your work. For each exercise, describe as many ways as possible to solve and to check in addition to the ones you used, and explain why each method works.

    For each polynomial give the standard form:

    a. $(2x^2 + x - 5) + (4x^2 - 3x) - (-3x^2 + x - 6)$ **b.** $(3x^2 + x - 2)(2x - 1)$

    c. $3(x^2 - 3x + 2) - 2(4x + 1)$ **d.** $(2x + 5)^2$

    Find and graph the solution sets:

    e. $x^2 - 16 < 0$ **f.** $2x^2 + x - 3 \geq 0$ **g.** $x^2 + 3x - 1 = 0$

    Give factored forms of the following function rules:

    h. $f(x) = 12x^3 - 8x$ **i.** $g(x) = x^2 - 64$ **j.** $h(x) = x^2 + 3x - 28$

2. Write a report that begins with a discussion of what it means for two algebraic expressions to be equivalent and what it means for a set of numbers to be a solution for an equation or inequality. Then present the paper-and-pencil solutions and checks that you used in Part 1 and your descriptions and explanations of the other methods that could be used to solve or to check solutions. Be sure to emphasize in your descriptions and explanations why your methods make sense in light of the meanings of equivalent expressions and solutions.

Units 1 – 3

Multiple Algebraic Methods

This project can be done by pairs or small groups of students. The purpose is for students to synthesize all of the algebraic methods available to them for simplifying, solving, and checking. It is important that students are aware of all the possibilities, as this increases their potential for success when faced with a particular problem. Identifying and comparing the range of methods also requires and makes use of an understanding of the meanings of the algebraic symbols and procedures. Too often, students see the manipulation of algebraic symbols as arbitrary and devoid of any meaning beyond a set of rules to be memorized for a test. Projects like this one help students develop and maintain a meaningful view of these procedures and skills.

1. a. $9x^2 - 3x + 1$
b. $6x^3 - x^2 - 5x + 2$

c. $3x^2 - 17x + 4$
d. $4x^2 + 20x + 25$

e. $-4 < x < 4$
f. $x < -\frac{3}{2}$ or $x > 1$
g. $x = \frac{-3 \pm \sqrt{13}}{2}$

h. $4x(3x^2 - 2)$
i. $(x + 8)(x - 8)$
j. $(x + 7)(x - 4)$

Suggested Timelines

Give students a day or two to solve all the problems; then check to see if the solutions, checks, and explanations are accurate. Once you are satisfied that they are on the right track, give students another few days to submit a rough draft of the report. If the draft shows major misconceptions or incomplete or inaccurate methods or it requires any other editing, return it with your feedback and give a second deadline for submitting the report in its final form. Students should have from several days to a week to submit the first draft and, if necessary, a few more days for the final report.

Report Format

The paper-and-pencil methods that were included in this unit certainly should be in the report. This includes the use of number properties and the properties of operations, factoring, and the quadratic formula. With the calculator, graph and table methods can be used to solve equations and inequalities and to check equivalence or solutions. The connection between x-intercepts and factors is useful for finding and checking factorizations. Numerically checking solutions, or sample solutions in the case of inequalities, is another calculator (or, in simple cases, paper-and-pencil) method for checking. It is particularly important that students show strong evidence that they understand that two expressions are equivalent, provided that they are equal when evaluated for any x. This implies, of course, that tables of values and graphs are identical.

Suggested Evaluation Criteria

1.	Format of the report follows directions	10%
2.	Accurate characterization of "equivalent expressions" and "solution sets"	20%
3.	Accurate solutions, checks, and explanations for given exercises	25%
4.	Complete list of alternative methods	25%
5.	Accurate and clear explanations of alternative methods	20%

Units 1–3

Exam Tasks

Since procedures and time frames for midterm and final examinations vary so much from school to school, we provide a variety of assessment tasks from which you can choose. You should choose tasks and construct an exam that fits your particular class needs and emphases. To help you choose, a brief summary of each task follows.

1. This task is an applied setting that assesses students' ability to use and manipulate a formula in three variables. Students evaluate the isolated variable when values of the other two variables are known. Students next write an equivalent formula that isolates a specified variable, and then they evaluate the equivalent formula. (Unit 1: *Multiple-Variable Models*)

2. This task presents students with inequalities that define a feasible region (in linear programming). Students graph the feasible region and use a given profit function to find the (x, y) point in the feasible region for which profit is maximized. (Unit 1: *Multiple-Variable Models*)

3. In this task, students are given the inequalities for a linear programming task; then they are asked to interpret the meaning, find an intersection point, write the profit equation, and find the maximum profit. (Unit 1: *Multiple-Variable Models*)

4. This task asks students to describe a region by stating the inequalities that define it. (Unit 1: *Multiple-Variable Models*)

5. This task requires students to use the Law of Cosines to solve for the length of one side of a triangle. (Unit 1: *Multiple-Variable Models*)

6. This task involves a voting situation in which votes are given by ranking, and students need to apply several different voting methods to determine a winner. A variation of the situation requires students to interpret the meaning of margin of error in a survey. (Unit 2: *Modeling Public Opinion*)

7. This task requires students to interpret a 90% box plot, compare it to a 90% confidence interval, and explain the meaning of a 3% margin of error in a survey. (Unit 2: *Modeling Public Opinion*)

8. This task requires students to compute and interpret particular values of a profit function $P(x)$, describe a practical domain and range and the theoretical domain and range of the function, and solve the equation for the ticket price that results in a particular profit. (Unit 3: *Symbol Sense and Algebraic Reasoning*)

9. This task requires students to describe what would happen to the range, mean, and median of a distribution of test scores if 50 points were added to each score and if each score were multiplied by 2. (Unit 3: *Symbol Sense and Algebraic Reasoning*)

10. This task assesses students' skill at various algebraic procedures when they are presented with no applied context. (Units 1 and 3: *Multiple-Variable Models and Symbol Sense and Algebraic Reasoning*)

© 1999 Everyday Learning Corporation

11. This task requires students to explain the connections between quadratic function rules, zeroes, lines of symmetry, and maximum and minimum values. (Unit 3: *Symbol Sense and Algebraic Reasoning*)

12. This task requires students to solve a quadratic equation by reasoning with the symbolic form and also by using technology. (Unit 3: *Symbol Sense and Algebraic Reasoning*)

Units 1 – 3

Units 1-3 Exam Tasks

Midterm

1. Towne Sporting Goods establishes a selling price S for an item based on the cost C that it paid the manufacturer and the rate R of markup that it charges in order to cover its expenses and make a profit. These variables are related by the following equation:

$$S = C(1 + R)$$

   a. Towne Sporting Goods gets a pair of in-line skates from the manufacturer at a cost of \$80. If Towne uses a 28% markup, what is the selling price of the skates to the nearest dollar?

   b. Use the equation $S = C(1 + R)$ to write an equivalent equation that gives C as a function of S and R.

   c. After the holidays, Towne Sporting Goods had a sale during which it sold all items in the store for a markup of 10%. The sale price of a tennis racket was \$32. To the nearest dollar, at what cost did Towne get the racket from the manufacturer?

    Use after page 257.

Units 1-3 Exam Tasks

Midterm

2. In a linear programming situation, the feasible region is defined by the following inequalities:

$$x + y \le 12$$
$$x + 3y \le 30$$
$$0 \le x \le 6$$
$$y \ge 0$$

a. Sketch a graph of the feasible region.

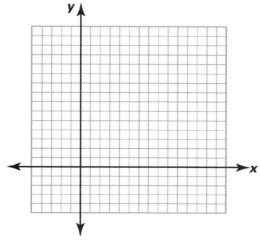

b. Using the profit function $P = 3x + 14y$, find (x, y) combinations that yield maximum profit within the feasible region.

Units 1 – 3

Units 1-3 Exam Tasks

Midterm

Units 1 – 3

3. Jones Industries, Inc. manufactures conventional and microwave ovens. Its two products are of such high quality that the company can sell as many as it can make, but the production capacity is limited in the areas of machining, welding, and assembly. Each week Jones Industries has available no more than 600 hours for machining, no more than 300 hours for welding, and no more than 550 hours for assembly. The number of hours required for production of a single item is shown below.

Production Requirments

Product	Machining	Welding	Assembly
Conventional Ovens	6	2	5
Microwave Ovens	4	3	5

This information can be modeled by the following system, in which x is the number of conventional ovens produced and y is the number of microwave ovens produced.

$$6x + 4y \leq 600$$
$$2x + 3y \leq 300$$
$$5x + 5y \leq 550$$

a. What is the meaning of the second inequality?

b. Identify the equations of the lines shown on the graph below.

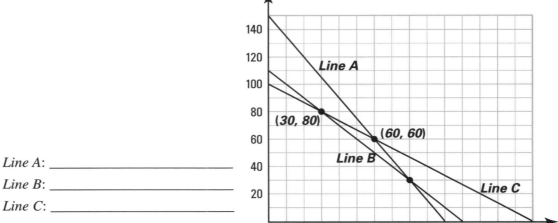

Line A: _____

Line B: _____

Line C: _____

c. The profit from the sale of a conventional oven is $90, and the profit from the sale of a microwave oven is $70.

■ Write an equation for the total profit from the sale of x conventional ovens and y microwave ovens.

■ Identify the feasible region for this situation on the graph.

■ Find the best combination of conventional and microwave ovens to make and sell in order to maximize profit.

4. The shaded region shown below is bounded by four lines. Describe the region with a system of four inequalities.

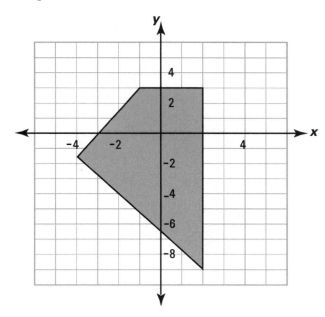

Units 1 – 3

5. The pitcher's mound on a softball field is 46 feet from home plate, and the distance between bases is 60 feet. The angle *PHF* is 45° as shown in the diagram. How far is the pitcher's mound from first base? (Note: You cannot assume that $\angle HPF$ is a right angle.)

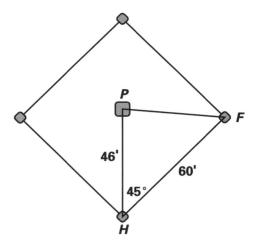

6. The Caledonia High School newspaper staff wanted to write an article about the issues of concern to high school seniors. They decided to have all seniors vote for the issue that was of greatest concern to them. Three issues, identified in a national survey, were included on the ballot and students voted for their first, second, and third preferences. The outcome of the voting is shown in the preference table below.

Issues Preference Table

	Rankings			
The Enivronment	1	2	3	1
The Economy	2	1	2	3
Future Education	3	3	1	2
Number of Voters	47 voters	149 voters	216 voters	168 voters

a. Using the plurality method, which issue, if any, is the winner? Explain.

b. Using the runoff method, which issue, if any, is the winner? Explain.

c. Using the pairwise-comparison method, which issue, if any, is the winner? Explain.

d. Using the points-for-preferences method, which issue, if any, is the winner? Explain.

e. The national survey mentioned in the problem found that 50% of adults (with a margin of error of 2%) indicated that the economy was their greatest concern. (Source: Krantz, Les. *America by the Numbers*. Boston: Houghton Mifflin Company, 1993.) Explain what it means for this survey to have a margin of error of 2%.

Units 1 – 3

Units 1-3 Exam Tasks

Midterm

7. According to a political poll by NBC News reported on *NBC Nightly News,* January 27, 1998, 60% of American adults approved of the job President Clinton was doing at the time of the poll. Below is a 90% box plot that shows the results of simulating a large number of random samples of 40 American adults and recording in each sample the number of people who approved of the job President Clinton was doing.

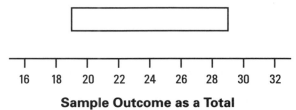

Sample Outcome as a Total

   a. Suppose you simulated a new random sample of 40 American adults in this situation and found that 30 approved of the job President Clinton was doing. Is your result likely or unlikely according to the given box plot? Explain.

   b. Is it correct to call the given box plot a 90% confidence interval? Why or why not?

   c. Suppose the poll had a margin of error of 3%. Explain what this means.

Use after page 257.

Units 1-3 Exam Tasks

Midterm

8. Based on data from past Johnson County Fairs, the predicted profit for a tractor-pulling contest as a function of x, the price per ticket in dollars, is

$$P(x) = -37x^2 + 890x - 2,300.$$

   a. Calculate and explain the meaning of $P(5)$ and $P(7)$ in terms of profit and ticket price.

   b. Describe a practical domain and practical range for the function $P(x)$.

   c. Describe the theoretical domain and range for the function $P(x)$.

   d. The solutions of the equation $2,500 = -37x^2 + 890x - 2,300$ answer a question about profit and ticket prices. What is that question?

   e. Solve the equation in Part d using any method. Explain your method. Then briefly describe a second method for solving the equation.

Units 1 – 3

Units 1-3 Exam Tasks

Midterm

9. Scores on a mathematics test ranged from 21 to 47, with a mean of 38 on a scale of 0 to 50. The teacher wanted to change the scoring scale so that it would be based on 100 instead of 50 points.

    a. What would the range and mean score be if the teacher added 50 points to each score?

    b. What would the range and mean score be if the teacher multiplied each test score by 2?

    c. How would the changes in Parts a and b affect the median, which was 36 on the original score scale?

Use after page 257.

Units 1-3 Exam Tasks

Midterm

10. The following items test your skill at various algebraic procedures. Show or explain your work in each case.

    a. Solve for x: $2x + 126 = 84 - 12x$

    b. Write in standard polynomial form: $(x - 3)(2x + 5)$

    c. Solve for x in terms of a, b, y, and t: $t = ax + by$

    d. Solve for y in terms of x and w: $w = \frac{x}{y}$

    e. Write in standard polynomial form: $(2x^3 - x + 5) - 3(x^3 + x^2 - 2)$

Units 1 – 3

Units 1-3 Exam Tasks

f. Solve for x: $-(x - 2)(x + 5) \geq 0$. Graph the solution.

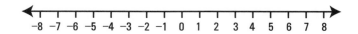

g. Write in standard polynomial form: $f(x) = (x - 1)(x^2 + 3x)$

h. Write in factored form: $f(x) = 2x^2 - 20x + 42$

i. Solve for x: $\dfrac{7}{\sin 32°} = \dfrac{12}{\sin x}$

Use after page 257.

Units 1-3 Exam Tasks

11. A particular quadratic function has two zeroes, 4 and -7.

    a. What information do you know about the graph of the function?

    b. Write the equation for the line of symmetry of the quadratic function.

    c. What information do you know about the maximum or minimum value of the function that has zeroes 4 and -7?

    d. Write one possible function rule for this function.

    e. Does your function have a maximum or minimum value? How does the function rule inform you of this?

Units 1-3 Exam Tasks

Midterm

12. $2x^2 - 7x + 6 = 0$

   a. Solve for x using symbolic reasoning alone.

   b. Solve for x using a method which employs technology.

   c. Explain how you can solve the equation in two other ways, one by symbolic reasoning and one with technology.

Units 1 – 3

Use after page 257.

Suggested Solutions

1. **a.** $S = 80(1 + 0.28) = 102.4$; the selling price is $102.40.

    b. Divide both sides of $S = C(1 + R)$ by $1 + R$. The result is $C = \frac{S}{1 + R}$.

    c. $C = \frac{32}{1 + 0.1} = \frac{32}{1.1} \approx \$29$.

2. **a.** The feasible region is the unshaded region. Scales on both axes are 1 unit per grid line. Vertices are labeled for reference in Part b.

    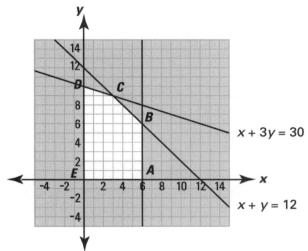

    b. The maximum profit will occur at one of the five vertices of the feasible region. The vertices of the feasible region are A (6, 0), B (6, 6), C (3, 9), D (0, 10), and E (0, 0). Point C (3, 9) will yield a higher value of P than any of the other vertices. At (3, 9), $P = 3(3) + 14(9) = 135$, the maximum profit.

3. **a.** $2x + 3y \leq 300$ represents the welding time of 2 hours for each of x conventional ovens and 3 hours for each of y microwave ovens. Total welding time must be no more than 300 hours.

    b. Line A: $6x + 4y = 600$
            Line B: $5x + 5y = 550$
            Line C: $2x + 3y = 300$

    c. ■ $P = 90x + 70y$
            ■

    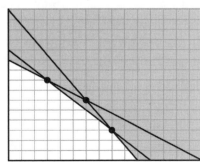

    ■ The maximum profit of $9,300 occurs at (80, 30).

Suggested Solutions *(continued)*

4. ■ $y \leq 3$

   ■ $x \leq 2$

   ■ $y \leq \frac{3}{2}x + \frac{9}{2}$

   ■ $y \geq -\frac{5}{4}x - \frac{13}{2}$

5. Using the Law of Cosines, you get the following:

$$PF^2 = 46^2 + 60^2 - 2(46)(60)\cos 45°$$
$$PF^2 \approx 1{,}812.8$$
$$PF \approx 42.58 \text{ feet}$$

6. **a.** Using the plurality method, Future Education is the winner with 216 votes. It has more first-preference votes than any other issue.

   b. The runoff is between Future Education and the Environment. The winner is the Environment $(364-216)$.

   c. There is no pairwise-comparison winner. The Environment beats Future Education $(364-216)$, the Economy beats the Environment $(365-215)$, and Future Education beats the Economy $(384-196)$.

   d. Giving 3 points for first preference, 2 points for second, and 1 point for third, the points-for-preferences winner is Future Education $(1{,}180)$, followed by the Environment $(1{,}159)$ and the Economy $(1{,}141)$.

   e. It is 90% (or another specific percent) certain that the actual percentage of adults who indicate that the economy is their biggest concern is between 48% and 52%. That is, 90% of all possible confidence intervals generated from all possible samples will contain the actual population percent. This is one of the possible confidence intervals, so we are 90% sure that it contains the actual population percent. (In a large national survey like this, it is likely that a 95% confidence level was used. However, since 90% confidence intervals were stressed in the unit for purposes of ease of computation, students should be allowed to answer this question using a 90% confidence level.)

7. **a.** The result is unlikely, since 30 is not in the 90% interval.

   b. No. A 90% confidence interval refers to a situation in which a population proportion is being estimated from sample outcomes, the reverse of the given situation.

   c. It is 90% certain that the actual percent of American adults who approved of the job that President Clinton was doing was between 57% and 63% (that is, 60% ± 3%).

8. **a.** $P(5) = 1{,}225$; $P(7) = 2{,}117$. These values are the predicted profits when the tickets are priced at $5 and $7, respectively.

   b. Assuming tickets will not be priced so that the tractor pull will lose money, the practical domain is about $2.94 \leq x \leq 21.11$. The practical range is then about $0 \leq y < 3{,}052.03$.

Units 1 – 3

Suggested Solutions *(continued)*

8. c. The theoretical domain is all real numbers, and the theoretical range is all numbers satisfying $y < 3{,}052.03$.

  d. What ticket prices give a predicted profit of $2,500?

  e. This equation can be solved using the quadratic formula, factoring (although that would be difficult in this case), graphing the profit function and then tracing to find the values of x for which P is 2,500, or using a table of values. Each of these methods should give solutions of about 8.17 and 15.89.

9. a. The range would be 26 (71 to 97), and the mean would be 88.

  b. The range would be 52 (42 to 94), and the mean would be 76.

  c. In Part a, the median would be 86. In Part b, it would be 72.

10. The solutions below use the standard paper-and-pencil approaches. Give credit for other correct approaches, including those that use the calculator.

  a. Subtract 84 from each side and subtract $2x$ from each side: $42 = -14x$. Then divide by -14: $x = -3$.

  b. Use the distributive property twice: $x(2x + 5) - 3(2x + 5) = 2x^2 + 5x - 6x - 15$. Then combine like terms: $2x^2 - x - 15$.

  c. Subtract by from each side: $ax = t - by$. Then divide by a: $x = \dfrac{t - by}{a}$.

  d. Multiply each side by y: $wy = x$. Then divide by w: $y = \dfrac{x}{w}$.

  e. Use the distributive property: $(2x^3 - x + 5) - 3x^3 - 3x^2 + 6$. Then combine like terms: $-x^3 - 3x^2 - x + 11$.

  f. $-(x - 2)(x + 5) = 0$ has solutions at $x = 2$ and $x = -5$, found by setting each factor equal to 0. So the solution to the inequality is $-5 \leq x \leq 2$.

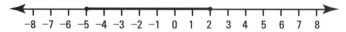

  g. Use the distributive property: $x(x^2 + 3x) - 1(x^2 + 3x)$. And use it again: $x^3 + 3x^2 - x^2 - 3x$. Then combine like terms: $x^3 + 2x^2 - 3x$.

  h. First factor out 2, the common factor: $2(x^2 - 10x + 21)$. Then factor the trinomial: $2(x - 7)(x - 3)$.

  i. $7\sin x = 12\sin 32°$

$$\sin x = \frac{12\sin 32°}{7}$$
$$x \approx \sin^{-1} 0.9084$$
$$x \approx 65.3°$$

Units 1 – 3

Suggested Solutions *(continued)*

11.   **a.** The graph is a parabola that crosses the x-axis at -7 and 4.

   b. $x = -\frac{3}{2}$

   c. The maximum or minimum value is $f\left(-\frac{3}{2}\right)$.

   d. Student rules should be of the form $f(x) = a(x - 4)(x + 7)$.

   e. If $a > 0$, then the function has a minimum value. If $a < 0$, then the function has a maximum value.

12.   **a.** Students could either factor or use the quadratic formula to obtain $x = 2$ or $x = 1.5$.

   b. Students could graph the quadratic equation and find the zeroes by tracing or by using the CALC roots or zero option on the calculator.

   c. See Parts a and b.

Units 1 – 3

Looking Back Over Course 3

Purpose

Each unit you have completed ends with a lesson called "Looking Back." The purpose of those lessons is to review and practice the most important ideas of the unit. Each lesson contains real-world problem situations. The problem situations in "Looking Back" lessons are similar to some of those in the unit, but, in some cases, they make use of ideas from across the entire unit rather than from just one lesson. In this project, you will be examining those "Looking Back" lessons, identifying the important ideas of each unit, and using what you learn as a guide to write some problem situations that would be appropriate for a "Looking Back" lesson over all three of the units.

Directions

1. Following are the unit objectives for student learning, which you will need to refer to in this project.

    Unit 1: *Multiple-Variable Models*

    ■ To develop an understanding of problems involving multiple-variable relations (including trigonometric relations) where one equation relates more than two variables

    ■ To develop the ability to solve multiple-variable equations for one variable in terms of the other variables

    ■ To model situations with systems of equations and inequalities where two or more output variables are related to the same input variable, and to apply those systems to solve problems

    Unit 2: *Modeling Public Opinion*

    ■ To measure and analyze public opinion through a mathematical analysis of voting and surveys

    ■ To use and analyze a variety of election analysis methods, particularly those based on preferential voting

    ■ To understand and apply basic ideas related to the design and interpretation of surveys, such as background information, random sampling, and bias

    ■ To construct simulated sampling distributions of sample proportions, and to use sampling distributions to identify which proportions are likely to be found in a sample of a given size

    ■ To construct and interpret margin of error and confidence intervals for population proportions

    ■ To critically analyze surveys and election in everyday life and as reported in the media

Unit 3

Project

Looking Back Over Course 3 *(continued)*

Unit 3: *Symbol Sense and Algebraic Reasoning*

- ■ To develop a more formal understanding of functions and function notation

- ■ To reason about algebraic expressions by applying the basic algebraic properties of commutativity, associativity, identity, inverse, and distributivity

- ■ To develop greater facility with algebraic operations with polynomials, including adding, subtracting, multiplying, factoring, and solving

- ■ To solve linear and quadratic equations and inequalities by reasoning with their symbolic forms

- ■ To prove important mathematical patterns by writing algebraic expressions, equations, and inequalities in equivalent forms and applying algebraic reasoning

2. Review the "Looking Back" lesson at the end of Unit 1. Indicate which of the objectives of the unit are being addressed in each problem situation and in the Checkpoint.

3. Repeat Activity 2 for the "Looking Back" lesson at the end of Unit 2. In addition, note any parts of the problem situations or Checkpoint in the Unit 2 "Looking Back" lesson in which an objective from Unit 1 is also addressed.

4. Repeat Activity 2 for the "Looking Back" lesson in Unit 3. In this case, note any parts of the problem situations or Checkpoint in which objectives from Units 1–3 are addressed.

5. Using the "Looking Back" activities in the three units as a guide, write two or more problem situations that would be appropriate for a "Looking Back" lesson over all three units. Each problem you write should address at least one objective from each of the units. Furthermore, your problems together should address each unit objective at least once.

6. Write a report that includes (a) your matching of the unit objectives to the "Looking Back" activities and Checkpoints, (b) the problem situations and questions that you write for the "Looking Back" over all three units, and (c) your matching of the unit objectives to the problem situations that you wrote.

Looking Back Over Course 3

If your students have not done any take-home assessments up to this point in the course, it is strongly recommended that you to try one of these two projects. Doing mathematics includes the global sorts of applications and the communication that these projects require.

This activity can be done by pairs or small groups of students, since students can discuss their decisions when they match objectives to questions. This project can be used as an assessment to which you assign a grade, or you may prefer to use it as a way to review Units 1–3. One important goal of the project is to help students better see the connections among the ideas in the first three units. The project is not just meant to review each unit separately. If more than one group work on this project, the groups should be given the opportunity to share and discuss their reports across the groups as this will allow them to see other approaches to the project.

Suggested Timeline

Students should probably have a day or two to complete Tasks 2–4. Once completed, they should turn in their work for your reaction and input. It is important that they are reading and matching the objectives accurately to the end-of-unit problems before they write their own problems. Next, they should have two or three days to write problems to which you should also provide feedback. Finally, the report itself should be easy if they have completed all parts up to this point. Another two days should be plenty of time.

Report Format

- The unit objectives should match the "Looking Back" problems and Checkpoints.
- Students' problem situations and how they match to objectives across the three units should be included.
- Students should write at least one problem that meets an objective in each of the three units should be included.

Suggested Evaluation Criteria

1. Format of the report follows directions   10%
2. Objectives are accurately matched to "Looking Back" problems   30%
3. Students' problems are interesting and well-written and meet unit objectives   50%
4. At least one problem meets an objective in each unit   10%

Algebra and the Calculator

Purpose

In Units 1 and 3, you learned how to manipulate algebraic expressions of several types. It is important that you develop a reasonable amount of skill doing this, but the calculator can also provide ways to do or check these manipulations. Using both the calculator and paper-and-pencil techniques for symbol manipulation can help to reinforce the connections between symbolic, graphic, and numeric representations of algebraic ideas. In this project, you will review several types of algebraic manipulations, recall how to carry them out without a calculator, and then review, or perhaps devise, ways that the calculator can be used to do or check the manipulations.

Directions

1. Complete each of these exercises without using a calculator. Then describe how the table and graph function of the calculator can be used either to do the exercise in another way or to check your solution. Write the descriptions carefully; they will be submitted as part of a written project report.

   a. Solve for x: $2x + 126 = 84 - 12x$

   b. Write in standard polynomial form: $(x - 3)(2x + 5)$

   c. Solve for x in terms of a, b, y, and t: $t = ax + by$

   d. Solve for y in terms of x and w: $w = \frac{x}{y}$

   e. Write in standard polynomial form: $(2x^3 - x + 5) - 3(x^3 + x^2 - 2)$

   f. Solve for x: $-(x - 2)(x + 5) \geq 0$

   g. Write in standard polynomial form: $f(x) = (x - 1)(x^2 + 3x)$

   h. Write in factored form: $f(x) = 2x^2 - 20x + 42$

2. For the remainder of your report, summarize the two or three different ways that you used the calculator in Task 1. In each case, explain why the calculator procedure works.

Unit 3

Algebra and the Calculator

If your students have not done any take-home assessments up to this point in the course, it is strongly recommended that you to try one of these two projects. Doing mathematics includes the global sorts of applications and the communication that these projects require. **Note:** The problems in this project are identical to Midterm Exam Item 10.

This project can best be done by pairs of students, since they can collaborate to find ways that the calculator can be used and verify why those ways work. This project can be used as an assessment to which you assign a grade, or you may prefer to use it as a way to review the connections between the algebraic techniques and the calculator. Important goals of the project are to ensure that students know how to use the calculator to solve equations, how to check whether two algebraic expressions are equivalent, and how to find equations of lines given certain standard conditions. If more than one pair work on this project, they should be given the opportunity to compare the ways they used the calculator and explore the reasons those ways work.

Suggested Timeline

There should be a two- or three-day deadline for solving the problems and finding ways to make use of the calculator. Have students submit this first part of the report and verify with you that they have found many of the ways the calculator can be used. Allow another two or three days for them to write the summary and reasons why the calculator methods work. Part of the purpose is to reinforce the students' understanding of the connections among the symbolic, graphic, and numeric representations of the algebraic ideas, so you may want to give them feedback on a draft before the final deadline to ensure that they are seeing these connections.

Report Format

■ The exercises should be solved correctly and completely without a calculator.

■ At least one way to use the calculator to solve or check each exercise should be described.

■ The main uses of the calculator should be summarized with reasons describing why each works.

Suggested Evaluation Criteria

1. Format of the report follows directions   10%

2. Exercises solved correctly and completely   40%

3. Accurate summary of the uses of the calculator   20%

4. Accurate and complete reasons for why the calculator methods work   30%

Unit 3

Lesson 1 Quiz

1. In Investigation 4, you proved that the angles of a triangle sum to 180°. Decide whether each of the following statements is correct or not. If a statement is not correct, give a counterexample. If it is correct, provide a proof.

   a. The sum of two angles of a triangle is greater than the third angle.

   b. If one angle of a triangle is obtuse, then the other two are acute.

    Use after page 296.

© 1999 Everyday Learning Corporation

Unit 4

Lesson 1 Quiz

c. In $\triangle ABC$ below, $m\angle 1 = m\angle A + m\angle B$.

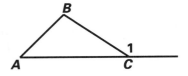

d. A triangle can have two right angles.

2. Explain the difference between inductive and deductive reasoning.

Unit 4

Suggested Solutions

1. **a.** Not correct. A counterexample is a triangle with angles with measures of 25°, 25° and 130°.

    b. Correct. If one angle is obtuse, its measure is greater than 90°. If either of the others were as much as 90°, the sum of the two obtuse angles would be greater than 180°. Therefore, both of the other angles must be less than 90°, that is, acute.

    c. Correct. $m\angle 1 + m\angle ACB = m\angle A + m\angle B + m\angle ACB$, since both sides of the equation sum to 180°. Subtracting $m\angle ACB$ from both sides gives $m\angle 1 = m\angle A + m\angle B$.

    d. Not correct. Two right angles sum to 180°, but the third angle of a triangle must have positive measure. So if the angles of a triangle sum to 180°, there can be no triangle with two right angles.

2. Reasoning from patterns based on analysis of specific cases is called inductive reasoning. Such reasoning may lead to an if-then statement that is plausible. However, deductive reasoning involves reasoning from facts, definitions, and accepted properties to new statements using principles of logic. Correct deductive reasoning leads to conclusions that are logically necessary, not just plausible.

Unit 4

Lesson 1 Quiz

1. In Investigation 4, you proved that the angles of a triangle sum to 180°. Decide whether each of the following statements is correct or not. If a statement is not correct, give a counterexample. If it is correct, provide a proof.

   a. If a triangle has three equal angles, then each measures 60°.

   b. If one angle of a triangle is a right angle, then the other two are acute.

Unit 4

c. In △ABC, below, m∠1 = m∠A + m∠C.

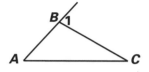

d. A triangle can have two obtuse angles.

2. Assume that the following statement is true: "If $\overleftrightarrow{AB} \perp \overleftrightarrow{CD}$ and $\overleftrightarrow{EF} \perp \overleftrightarrow{CD}$, then $\overleftrightarrow{AB} \parallel \overleftrightarrow{EF}$." Suppose $\overleftrightarrow{AB} \parallel \overleftrightarrow{EF}$. Does it follow logically from the true statement that $\overleftrightarrow{AB} \perp \overleftrightarrow{CD}$ and $\overleftrightarrow{EF} \perp \overleftrightarrow{CD}$? Explain.

Suggested Solutions

1. **a.** Correct. Since the three angles sum to 180° and they are equal to one another, each must be $\frac{1}{3}$ (180°) or 60°.

    b. Correct. If one angle is a right angle, its measure is 90°. If either of the other angles were as much as 90°, the sum of these two alone would be at least 180°. Therefore, both of the other angles must be less than 90°, that is, acute.

    c. Correct. $m\angle 1 + m\angle ABC = m\angle A + m\angle ABC + m\angle C$, since both sides of the equation sum to 180°. Subtracting $m\angle ABC$ from both sides, gives $m\angle 1 = m\angle A + m\angle C$.

    d. Not correct. An obtuse angle, by definition, has a measure greater than 90°, so the sum of the measures of two obtuse angles is greater than 180°. This contradicts the fact that the sum of the measures of the three angles of a triangle is 180°.

2. No. Since the converse of an if-then is logically independent of the statement itself, it does not follow logically that $\overleftrightarrow{AB} \perp \overleftrightarrow{CD}$ and $\overleftrightarrow{EF} \perp \overleftrightarrow{CD}$ if $\overleftrightarrow{AB} \parallel \overleftrightarrow{EF}$. A separate proof of the converse of a statement is needed to accept it as true.

Unit 4

Lesson 2 Quiz

Form A

1. A soldiers' monument with a 4-foot square base at City Park always appeared to Nell to be about the same height as a telephone pole, which she knew from her summer job with the phone company was 28 feet. One bright, sunny day, Nell thought of a way to check her observation. She decided to measure the lengths of the shadows of the monument and a telephone pole.

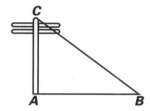 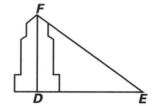

   a. Nell measured the lengths of the shadows (*AB* and *DE*) and found that they were both about 18 feet long. She assumed that the acute angle made by the sun's rays and the ground was the same in each of the triangles above. What else would she need to assume in order to conclude that the monument was also 28 feet high?

   b. Later, Nell realized that she should have added two feet to her measurement of the monument's shadow to account for the width of its base. With this correction, the monument's shadow was 20 feet long, while the telephone pole's shadow was 18 feet long. Find the height of the monument after making this correction. (Assume angle measures remain the same.) Show or explain your work.

Lesson 2 Quiz

2. Refer to the figure below.

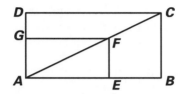

a. Name two pairs of triangles that appear to be congruent and two pairs that appear to be similar (but not congruent).

Congruent triangles:

Similar triangles:

b. In the figure, $\overleftrightarrow{CD} \parallel \overleftrightarrow{AB}$ and $\overline{CD} \cong \overline{AB}$. Prove that $\overline{AD} \cong \overline{BC}$.

Suggested Solutions

1. **a.** She would need to assume that the pole and the monument were both vertical, the ground was level, and her measurement in each case was from a point directly below the top. These conditions would ensure that the angle at the base of each structure was a right angle.

   b. Since each triangle has a right angle and a pair of equal acute angles, the triangles are similar. Their scale factor is $\frac{18}{20}$ or 0.9, so the height of the monument is $\frac{28}{0.9}$ or approximately 31.1 ft.

2. **a.** Congruent triangles: $\triangle ABC$ and $\triangle ADC$; $\triangle AEF$ and $\triangle AGF$
   Similar triangles: $\triangle ABC$ and $\triangle AEF$; $\triangle ADC$ and $\triangle AGF$ (also $\triangle ABC$ and $\triangle AGF$; $\triangle ADC$ and $\triangle AEF$)

   b. Since $\overleftrightarrow{CD} \parallel \overleftrightarrow{AB}$, $m\angle ACD = m\angle BAC$ (alternate interior angles). $\overline{AC} \cong \overline{AC}$ and we know that $\overline{CD} \cong \overline{AB}$, so $\triangle ABC \cong \triangle ADC$ by the SAS Congruence Theorem. It follows that $\overline{AD} \cong \overline{BC}$ (corresponding parts of congruent triangles).

Unit 4

Lesson 2 Quiz

Form B

1. Two surveyors planned to measure the distance *MN* across Grand Lake. They marked point *P* and measured *PM* and *PN* as indicated in the figure below.

Grand Lake

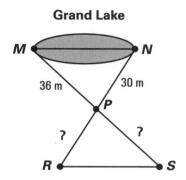

a. The first surveyor's plan was to extend segment *PM* to point *S* so that *PS* = 36 meters, extend segment *PN* to point *R* so that *PR* = 30 meters, and then measure *RS*. If *RS* = 45 meters, what is *MN*? Explain.

b. The second surveyor's plan was to extend segment *PM* to point *S* so that *PS* = 24 meters, extend segment *PN* to point *R* so that *PR* = 20 meters, and then measure *RS*. If *RS* measures 30 meters, would the surveyors be able to determine the length of *MN*? If yes, find the length of *MN* and explain how you know your answer is correct. If no, explain why not.

Unit 4

Lesson 2 Quiz

2. Refer to the figure below.

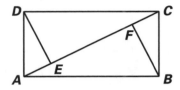

a. Name two pairs of triangles that appear to be congruent and two pairs that appear to be similar (but not congruent).

Congruent triangles:

Similar triangles:

b. In the figure, $\overleftrightarrow{AD} \parallel \overleftrightarrow{BC}$ and $\overline{AD} \cong \overline{BC}$. Prove that $\overline{AB} \cong \overline{DC}$.

Suggested Solutions

1. **a.** $MN = 45$ meters. Since m$\angle MPN$ = m$\angle SPR$ (vertical angles), $PM = PS$, and $PN = PR$, it follows that $\triangle MNP \cong \triangle SRP$ by the SAS Congruence Theorem. Thus, $MN = RS$ (CPCTC).

    b. Yes, they could find the length of MN (45 meters). Since $\frac{PS}{PM} = \frac{24}{36} = \frac{2}{3}$, $\frac{PR}{PN} = \frac{20}{30} = \frac{2}{3}$, and m$\angle MPN$ = m$\angle SPR$, it follows that $\triangle MNP \sim \triangle SRP$ by the SAS Similarity Theorem. Therefore, $RS = \frac{2}{3}(MN)$ or $MN = \frac{3}{2}(30) = 45$ meters.

2. **a.** Congruent triangles: $\triangle AED$ and $\triangle CFB$; $\triangle CED$ and $\triangle AFB$; $\triangle ACD$ and $\triangle CAB$ Similar triangles: $\triangle AED$ and $\triangle DEC$; $\triangle AED$ and $\triangle ADC$; $\triangle DEC$ and $\triangle ADC$; $\triangle CFB$ and $\triangle BFA$; $\triangle CFB$ and $\triangle CBA$; $\triangle AFB$ and $\triangle ABC$

    b. Since $\overleftrightarrow{AD} \parallel \overleftrightarrow{BC}$, m$\angle CAD$ = m$\angle ACB$ (alternate interior angles). $\overline{AC} \cong \overline{AC}$ and we know that $\overline{AD} \cong \overline{BC}$, so $\triangle ABC \cong \triangle CDA$ by the SAS Congruence Theorem. It follows that $\overline{AB} \cong \overline{CD}$ (corresponding parts of congruent triangles).

Unit 4

Lesson 3 Quiz

Form A

1. Use the following figure and definitions to answer Parts a and b.

   ■ A *rectangle* is a parallelogram that has one right angle.

   ■ A *rhombus* is a parallelogram with a pair of congruent adjacent sides.

   ■ A *square* is a rhombus with one right angle.

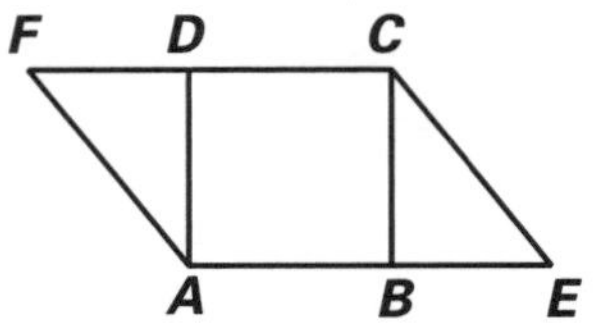

   a. Assume that *AECF* is a parallelogram and $\overline{BE} \cong \overline{DF}$.
   Does it follow that *ABCD* is:

A square?	*Yes* ___	*No* ___
A rectangle?	*Yes* ___	*No* ___
A rhombus?	*Yes* ___	*No* ___
A parallelogram?	*Yes* ___	*No* ___

   b. Assume *ABCD* and *AECF* are parallelograms. Prove that *BE* = *DF*.

Lesson 3 Quiz

2. For each of the following types of quadrilaterals, write the most specific property that holds true of its diagonals.

   a. Parallelogram

   b. Rectangle

   c. Rhombus

   d. Square

3. Prove any one of the four properties from Activity 2 above. You may use either a synthetic or an analytic (coordinate) proof.

Unit 4

Suggested Solutions

1. **a.** No, for all but a parallelogram.

    b. Quadrilaterals *ABCD* and *AECF* are both parallelograms, so opposite sides have equal lengths. In particular, $AE = FC$ and $AB = DC$. Thus,
    $$AE - AB = FC - AB$$
    $$AE - AB = FC - DC$$
    $$BE = DF$$

2. **a.** The diagonals of a parallelogram bisect each other.

    b. The diagonals of a rectangle bisect each other and are congruent.

    c. The diagonals of a rhombus are the perpendicular bisectors of one another.

    d. The diagonals of a square are the perpendicular bisectors of one another and are congruent.

3. All properties are proven in the investigations or MORE Tasks in the Teacher's Guide.

    a. See the Teacher's Guide, page T328 (Activity 4 Part f).

    b. See the Teacher's Guide, page T335 (Organizing Task 1 Parts b–d).

    c. See the Teacher's Guide, page T331 (Activity 1 Part d, second proof).

    d. See the Teacher's Guide, page T335 (Organizing Task 2 Part c).

Use after page 339.

Unit 4

Lesson 3 Quiz

1. Use the following figure and definitions to answer Parts a and b.

   ■ A *rectangle* is a parallelogram that has one right angle.

   ■ A *rhombus* is a parallelogram with a pair of congruent adjacent sides.

   ■ A *square* is a rhombus with one right angle.

   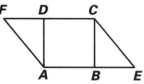

   a. Assume *AECF* is a parallelogram, $\overline{AD} \perp \overline{CF}$, and $\overline{BC} \perp \overline{AE}$. Does it follow that *ABCD* is:

A square?	*Yes* ___ *No* ___
A rectangle?	*Yes* ___ *No* ___
A rhombus?	*Yes* ___ *No* ___

   b. Assume *ABCD* is a square and $\overline{AF} \cong \overline{CE}$. Prove that *AECF* is a parallelogram.

Unit 4

Lesson 3 Quiz

2. For Parts a through d, assume *ABCD* is a quadrilateral with the given property. Place a check in each space if the property is a sufficient condition to conclude that *ABCD* is the indicated type of quadrilateral.

   a. $\overline{AC}$ and $\overline{BD}$ bisect each other.

   Parallelogram _____ *Square* _____ *Rectangle* _____ *Rhombus* _____

   b. $\overline{AC}$ and $\overline{BD}$ bisect each other and are congruent.

   Parallelogram _____ *Square* _____ *Rectangle* _____ *Rhombus* _____

   c. $\overline{AC}$ and $\overline{BD}$ are perpendicular bisectors of one another.

   Parallelogram _____ *Square* _____ *Rectangle* _____ *Rhombus* _____

   d. $\overline{AC}$ and $\overline{BD}$ are perpendicular bisectors of one another and are congruent.

   Parallelogram _____ *Square* _____ *Rectangle* _____ *Rhombus* _____

3. $\overline{FM} \cong \overline{HM}$ and $\overline{JM} \cong \overline{GM}$. Prove that $\overleftrightarrow{FG} \parallel \overleftrightarrow{JH}$. You may use either a synthetic or analytic (coordinate) proof.

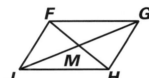

© 1999 Everyday Learning Corporation

Unit 4

Suggested Solutions

1. **a.** No, for all but a rectangle.

    b. Students may choose to do this proof in a variety of ways, by using right triangle congruence theorems if they have proved them in Organizing Task 3, page 312; the SSS Congruence Theorem; or other theorems. A sample proof follows.

    Since $ABCD$ is a square, $AD = BC = AB = CD$ and m$\angle ADF$ = m$\angle CBE$ = 90°. Thus, $\triangle ADF$ and $\triangle CBE$ are right triangles with a leg of one congruent to a leg of the other and congruent hypotenuses (given $\overline{AF} \cong \overline{CE}$). Therefore, the other legs are also congruent by the Pythagorean Theorem. $\triangle ADF \cong \triangle CBE$ by the SSS Congruence Theorem. So $DF = BE$ (corresponding parts of congruent triangles). Adding this last equation to $CD = AB$ gives $CD + DF = AB + BE$ or $CF = AE$. It follows that $AECF$ is a parallelogram, because two pairs of opposite sides are congruent.

2. **a.** Parallelogram

    b. Parallelogram, rectangle and square

    c. rhombus and square

    d. All four types

3. Using the given information and vertical angles, $\triangle JMH \cong \triangle GMF$ by the SAS Congruence Theorem. Thus $\angle FGJ$ and $\angle GJH$ are congruent. Since they are alternate interior angles, $\overleftrightarrow{FG} \parallel \overleftrightarrow{JH}$. A coordinate proof could be done by labeling J as $(0, 0)$, H as $(a, 0)$, and M as (b, c). Then use the distance formula and the given information that $\overline{FM} \cong \overline{HM}$ and $\overline{JM} \cong \overline{GM}$ to find the coordinates of F and G and show that the y-coordinate of each point is the same. Thus the slope of $\overleftrightarrow{FG}$ is the same as the slope of $\overleftrightarrow{JH}$, so $\overleftrightarrow{FG} \parallel \overleftrightarrow{JH}$.

Unit 4

In-Class Exam

Form A

1. In the figure shown at the right, *AD* = *BC*, *AC* = *BD*, and *DE* = *CE*.

    a. Several pairs of triangles appear to be congruent.
    Choose one of these pairs of triangles and prove
    that the triangles are congruent.

    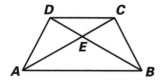

    b. Name a pair of triangles that appears to be similar but not congruent. Prove that these triangles
    are similar.

    c. Prove that $\overleftrightarrow{AB} \parallel \overleftrightarrow{CD}$.

Unit 4

In-Class Exam

2. The Law of Cosines and the Law of Sines can be used to find missing parts of triangles when at least three parts are given. In particular, the other parts of a triangle can be found if three sides are known (SSS), two sides and the included angle are known (SAS), or two angles and the included side are known (ASA). Explain how to find the lengths of the other sides and the measures of the other angles in each case below.

   a. SSS   **b.** SAS

   c. ASA

3. **a.** Suppose "If A, then B" is a true statement. In a particular situation, you know that B is false. Can you logically conclude that A is true? That A is false? Explain.

   b. What is the role of B in proving "If A, then B" is a correct statement?

Unit 4

4. In the figure at the right, *BEDF* is a rectangle, and *AE = CF*. Prove analytically (that is, using coordinates) that *ABCD* is a parallelogram.

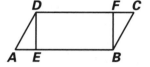

5. A surveyor calculated the distance across a lake using this sketch, in which $\overleftrightarrow{MN} \parallel \overleftrightarrow{RS}$. Assume the lengths of all segments in the figure except *MN* can be measured directly. Describe a plan that would allow the surveyor to determine the distance *MN* across the lake using direct measurements of other sides or angles.

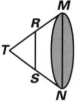

Suggested Solutions

1. **a.** One choice is $\triangle ACD$ and $\triangle BDC$. They are congruent by the SSS Congruence Theorem using the given information and $\overline{CD} \cong \overline{CD}$. Other pairs that may be chosen are $\triangle ABC$ and $\triangle BAD$ or $\triangle BCE$ and $\triangle ADE$.

    b. The only pair of similar triangles is $\triangle AEB$ and $\triangle CED$. Since $AC = BD$ and $DE = CE$, it follows by subtraction that $AE = BE$. Hence, $\frac{AE}{CE} = \frac{BE}{DE}$. Because vertical angles are congruent, $m\angle AEB = m\angle CED$. Therefore, $\triangle AEB \sim \triangle CED$ by the SAS Similarity Theorem.

    c. From Part b, $m\angle ACD = m\angle CAB$. Since a pair of alternate interior angles are congruent, $\overleftrightarrow{AB} \parallel \overleftrightarrow{CD}$.

2. **a.** Use the Law of Cosines to find the measure of one angle; then use either law (sines or cosines) to find the measure of a second angle. The third angle has measure 180° minus the sum of the measures of the other two.

    b. Use the Law of Cosines to find the length of the third side; then use either law (sines or cosines) to find the measure of the second angle. Finally, the measure of the third angle is 180° minus the sum of the measures of the other two.

    c. The measure of the third angle is 180° minus the sum of the measures of the given angles. Use the Law of Sines to find the length of a second side; then use either law (sines or cosines) to find the length of the third side.

3. **a.** We can conclude that A is false. Since "If *A*, then *B*" is true, this means that in every situation in which *A* is true, *B* is also true. In this particular situation, *B* is false. Therefore, *A* cannot be true, so it logically follows that *A* must be false.

    b. *B* is the statement that must be proven, assuming that *A* is true.

Unit 4

Suggested Solutions *(continued)*

4. Students might label their parallelograms in a variety of ways. Proofs should show that $\overline{AD} \parallel \overline{BC}$ because the slopes are identical. $\overline{DF} \parallel \overline{EB}$ since *BEDF* is a rectangle. Therefore, *ABCD* is a parallelogram by definition.

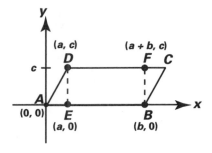

5. Since $\overleftrightarrow{MN} \parallel \overleftrightarrow{RS}$, $\triangle RTS \sim \triangle MTN$. Students should provide an explanation involving the proportional sides of similar triangles. For example, measure $\overline{RS}$; then measure $\overline{RT}$ and $\overline{MT}$ so that the proportion $\frac{MN}{RS} = \frac{MT}{RT}$ can be solved. The surveyor could measure $\overline{ST}$ and $\overline{NT}$ instead of $\overline{RT}$ and $\overline{MT}$ and solve the proportion $\frac{MN}{RS} = \frac{NT}{ST}$.

Unit 4

In-Class Exam

1. In the figure shown at the right, $\overleftrightarrow{AB} \parallel \overleftrightarrow{CD}$, and $\overline{BD}$ intersects $\overline{AC}$ at M, the midpoint of $\overline{AC}$. Prove that $\overline{AB} \cong \overline{DC}$.

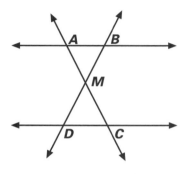

2. **a.** Explain why finding a counterexample to an if-then statement proves that the if-then statement is not true.

   b. How is A used in proving that "If A, then B" is a correct statement?

Unit 4

In-Class Exam

3. One parallelogram has sides with lengths 10, 8, 10, and 8. Another parallelogram has sides with respective lengths 15, 12, 15, and 12. Must the two parallelograms be similar? Why or why not?

4. In the diagram at the right, circles M and N intersect at A and B. Conjecture: $\triangle MAN \cong \triangle MBN$. Prove that the conjecture is correct or incorrect.

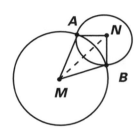

Unit 4

In-Class Exam

5. In the figure shown at the right, *ABCD* is a parallelogram, and $\angle BED$ and $\angle EBF$ are right angles. Prove synthetically (that is, without using coordinates) that *BEDF* is a rectangle.

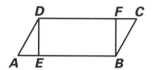

6. Quadrilateral *ABCD* is a parallelogram, and $\angle A$ is a right angle. Prove analytically (that is, using coordinates) that *AC = BD*.

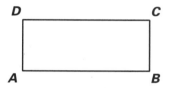

Unit 4

Suggested Solutions

1. $\angle BAM \cong \angle DCM$ since $\overleftrightarrow{AB} \parallel \overleftrightarrow{CD}$ (alternate interior angles). $\angle AMB \cong \angle CMD$ since they are vertical angles. $\overline{AM} \cong \overline{CM}$ since M is the midpoint of $\overline{AC}$. Thus, $\triangle AMB \cong \triangle CMD$ (ASA Congruence Theorem), and $\overline{AB} \cong \overline{CD}$ by corresponding parts.

2. **a.** A counterexample is a situation in which the hypothesis (the if part) of a conditional holds but the conclusion (the then part) does not. Thus, the conditional statement is not true.

    b. A is used as beginning information on which to base deductions. It is assumed or given to be correct.

3. No, the parallelograms are not necessarily similar since each is not rigid. In order for the parallelograms to be similar, one angle would need to be fixed; then the proportional sides would guarantee similarity.

4. The conjecture is correct. Since circles have equal radii, $AN = NB$ and $MA = MB$. Also $MN = MN$. So $\triangle MAN \cong \triangle MBN$ by the SSS Congruence Theorem.

5. Since $\angle BED$ and $\angle EBF$ are right angles, lines DE and BF are parallel. Since $ABCD$ is a parallelogram, it follows that lines AB (or BE) and CD (or DF) are parallel. Therefore, $BEDF$ is a parallelogram with a right angle. By definition, $BEDF$ is a rectangle.

6. Place the origin at point A. Since $ABCD$ is a parallelogram, opposite sides are parallel and equal. Therefore, the other vertices may be labeled as in the figure below. Using the distance formula,
    $$AC = \sqrt{(a-0)^2 + (b-0)^2} = \sqrt{a^2 + b^2} = \sqrt{(0-a)^2 + (b-0)^2} = BD.$$

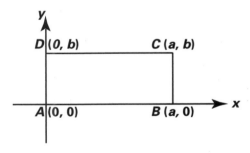

Unit 4

Take-Home Assessment

1. Two triangles are congruent if two sides and the included angle of one triangle are congruent to the corresponding parts in the second triangle. This theorem is abbreviated SAS. But what if the congruent angle is *not* included between the pairs of congruent sides? Complete the following activities that explore the question of whether there is an SSA Theorem for congruent triangles.

   a. Use a protractor and ruler to draw a triangle ABC in which $m\angle A = 40°$, $a = 3$ inches, and $c = 4$ inches.

   b. Measure the other parts of $\triangle ABC$ and compute them using the Law of Sines and Law of Cosines. Do your measurements agree with your computed results?

   c. Draw a second triangle that satisfies the conditions in Part a but that is not congruent to the first one you drew.

   d. Repeat Part b for the second triangle.

   e. Explain why Parts a through d illustrate that there can be no SSA theorem for congruent triangles.

2. In the rectangle at the right, $\frac{a}{b} = \frac{b}{a+b}$. Any rectangle that is similar to this one is called a *golden rectangle*. It is said that of all rectangles, a golden rectangle is most pleasing to the human eye. For this reason, golden rectangles appear frequently in art, architecture, and even products that have rectangular shapes.

   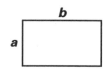

   a. Identify at least 10 rectangles around your home or school that are approximately golden rectangles. For example, consider tablets of paper, books, index cards, rectangular windows, pictures, floors or ceilings of rooms, cereal boxes, and so on.

   b. On the right, a golden rectangle is divided into a small rectangle and a square that is a units on a side. Prove that the small rectangle is also a golden rectangle. **Hint:** By cross multiplying, $\frac{a}{b} = \frac{b}{a+b}$ if and only if $a^2 + ab = b^2$. Use this result and a similar proportion for the small rectangle.

   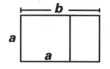

Unit 4

Take-Home Assessment

3. The ratio of the longer side to the shorter side of a golden rectangle is called the *golden ratio*. For example, in the golden rectangle shown in Task 2, the ratio $\frac{b}{a}$ is the golden ratio.

   a. Measure a and b in the rectangle given in Task 2, and use your measurements to estimate the numerical value of the golden ratio.

   b. The rhombus at the right has sides of length 1 inch. It is divided into four triangles with angle measures as shown. Use the Law of Sines or the Law of Cosines to compute the lengths x and y.

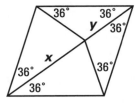

   c. Show that the ratio $\frac{x}{y}$ is approximately the golden ratio.

You may choose to assign one, two, or all three of these activities.

1. **a.** There are two possible triangles satisfying the given conditions, as shown at the right.

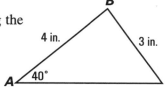 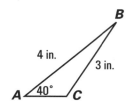

b. The following solution assumes that the student drew the figure on the left in Part a. The solution for the figure on the right is given in Part d. $\frac{3}{\sin 40°} = \frac{4}{\sin C}$; $m\angle C \approx 59°$. It follows that $m\angle B \approx 81°$. Then $b^2 = 3^2 + 4^2 - 2(3)(4)(\cos 81°)$, and $b \approx 4.6$ in. Measurements should approximate these values if the student drew on the left.

c. The drawing should be one of the triangles above in Part a.

d. If students try the same methods as in Part b, they again get that $m\angle C = 59°$, which is clearly not true. They should observe that $m\angle C \approx 180° - 59° = 121°$. Thus $m\angle B \approx 19°$. Using the Law of Cosines, $b \approx 1.5$ in. Measurements should approximate these values; measuring $\angle C$ may help students see that $m\angle C \approx 180° - 59°$.

e. Parts a through d show that SSA holds for both triangles in Part a, but these triangles are not congruent. This exercise is, therefore, a counterexample of an SSA Theorem.

Unit 4

2. **a.** Answers may vary. There are many possibilities.

    b. The width of the small rectangle is $b - a$, so the analogous proportion is $\frac{b-a}{a} = \frac{a}{b-a+a}$. To show that $\frac{b-a}{a} = \frac{a}{b}$, note that cross multiplying gives $a^2 = b^2 - ab$, which is equivalent to the known equation $a^2 + ab = b^2$.

3. **a.** The golden ratio is approximately 1.62. Allow some room for measurement error here.

    b. The other angles measure 108° or 72°. It follows that the two triangles in the lower left are isosceles, so $x = 1$ inch. $\frac{y}{\sin 36°} = \frac{1}{\sin 108°}$, so $y \approx 0.62$.

    c. $\frac{x}{y} \approx \frac{1}{0.62} \approx 1.62$

Unit 4

Project

Reasoning with Coordinates

Purpose

In earlier units (especially Unit 2, Course 2), you learned how to represent many geometric ideas with a coordinate system. The reasoning in the present unit focused on geometric relationships, but coordinates were rarely used. In this project, you will reason about geometric ideas using coordinates. The purpose is to strengthen the connection between coordinate and synthetic (non-coordinate) geometry.

Directions

In Lesson 3, a parallelogram was defined as a quadrilateral in which both pairs of opposite sides are parallel. Recall that in coordinate geometry, two lines are parallel provided that their slopes are equal. The simplest way to represent a parallelogram with coordinates is shown at the right.

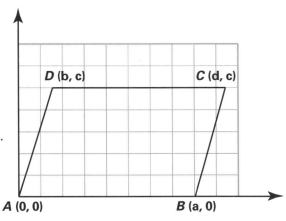

1. By definition, $\overleftrightarrow{AB} \parallel \overleftrightarrow{CD}$, so both vertices C and D can be labeled with the same y-coordinate, c. Explain why.

2. By definition, $\overleftrightarrow{AD} \parallel \overleftrightarrow{BC}$. Write d in terms of a and b and explain your reasoning.

3. Use the distance and midpoint formulas to prove the following:

   ■ Opposite sides of a parallelogram are congruent.

   ■ Diagonals of a parallelogram bisect each other.

   ■ Diagonals of a rectangle are congruent.

4. Recall how these same conclusions were reached without coordinates. Write a report that includes your responses to Tasks 1 through 3 and a few closing paragraphs in which you compare reasoning with coordinate proofs to reasoning without coordinates.

Unit 4

Reasoning with Coordinates

This project can be done by individual students or by pairs, as you prefer. You may want to provide a review of coordinate ideas, such as equal slopes for parallel lines, negative reciprocal slopes for perpendicular lines, the distance formula, and the midpoint formula. In addition to the purpose stated on the assignment sheet, this activity will provide students with further practice with symbolic expressions.

1. $\overleftrightarrow{AB} \parallel \overleftrightarrow{CD}$ implies that the slopes of lines AB and CD are equal, in this case, to 0. Thus, the y-coordinates should be equal.

2. $\overleftrightarrow{AD} \parallel \overleftrightarrow{BC}$ implies that the lines have equal slopes, that is, $\frac{c}{b} = \frac{c}{d-a}$. Hence, $b = d - a$ or $d = b + a$.

3. For the first statement, use the distance formula to compute the lengths of opposite sides to see that they are equal. For the second statement, find the midpoint of each diagonal to see that the two diagonals are equal. For the third statement, choose the coordinates of the vertices of the rectangle as $(0, 0)$, $(a, 0)$, (a, b), and $(0, b)$. Then compute the lengths of the diagonals.

4. Reactions to coordinate versus synthetic proofs will vary.

Suggested Timeline

Give students a day or two to try the activity, then check to see if they are understanding what needs to be done. Also, have students submit a rough draft of the report. If it shows major misconceptions or requires editing, return it with your feedback, and give students a second deadline for submitting the report in its final form. Students should have several days to a week to submit the first draft and, if necessary, a few more days for the final report.

Suggested Evaluation Criteria

1. Format of the report follows directions   20%

2. Accuracy of explanation in Task 1   10%

3. Accuracy of solution to Task 2   15%

4. Clarity and accuracy of proofs in Task 3   45%

5. Quality of comparison of coordinate and synthetic proofs   10%

Unit 4

Project

Symmetries and Other Properties

Purpose

In Course 1, Unit 5, you explored the symmetries of various geometric figures. A *symmetry* of a set of points is a translation, line reflection, rotation, or glide reflection that maps the set of points onto itself. In the unit you just completed, you proved various properties of geometric shapes. In this project, you will revisit some of these shapes and connect their symmetries with their properties.

Directions

1. Draw each of the following geometric figures: two parallel lines cut by a transversal, vertical angles, isosceles triangle, equilateral triangle, parallelogram, rectangle, rhombus, and square. Include both diagonals in the last four figures.

2. List all of the symmetries of each geometric figure you drew in Task 1.

3. List the properties of each geometric figure that were proved in this unit.

4. Discuss the ways in which the symmetries are related to the properties. For example, a pair of angles may be congruent (property), and one angle maps onto the other under a particular symmetry of the figure. Conversely, each symmetry should suggest some properties of angles or segments in the figure.

5. Write a report that includes the following for each geometric figure in Task 1: a drawing, a list of symmetries, a list of properties, and a discussion of how the symmetries and properties are related to one another. In the last section of your report, make some conjectures (and explain your reasoning) about how the symmetries of any geometric figure are related to its properties, that is, how certain symmetries imply certain properties and vice versa.

Unit 4

Symmetries and Other Properties

This project can probably be done best by a small group of students, since all can participate in drawing the figures, identifying symmetries and other properties, and discussing their connections. A review of the four transformations and the idea of symmetry from Course 1, Unit 5, may be necessary. It is especially important that students recognize that if any of these transformations maps a segment to a segment or an angle to an angle, the image and pre-image are congruent.

Important Points for the Report

A symmetry for two parallel lines cut by a transversal is a half turn about the midpoint of the segment of the transversal that lies between the parallel lines. This symmetry maps pairs of alternate interior angles onto one another. A half turn of two intersecting lines about the point of intersection maps opposite pairs of (vertical) angles onto each other. Reflection in the altitude from the vertex angle of an isosceles triangle is related to the fact that base angles are congruent and the altitude bisects the vertex angle. For equilateral triangles, any altitude suffices since all three angles are congruent, which also allows for a rotation of 60° about the centroid to be a symmetry. Properties of angles and diagonals can also be seen to be related to the symmetries of the various polygons that the students are to draw.

Suggested Timeline

Give students a day or two to try the activity; then check to see if they are understanding what needs to be done. Also, have students submit a rough draft of the report. If it shows major misconceptions or requires editing, return it with your feedback, and give students a second deadline for submitting the report in its final form. Students should have several days to a week to submit the first draft and, if necessary, a few more days for the final report. If you wish to reduce the time needed for this project, you can ask students to pick one geometric figure for their complete report. (See Task 5 on the assignment sheet.)

Suggested Evaluation Criteria

1.	Format of the report follows directions	10%
2.	Listing of symmetries is accurate and complete	25%
3.	Listing of properties is accurate and complete	25%
4.	Discussion of the relationship between symmetries and properties is accurate	20%
5.	Students clearly state the congruence of image and pre-image	20%

Use after page 344.

Unit 4